Mentoring Faculty
of Color

D0947775

Mentoring Faculty of Color

Essays on Professional Development
and Advancement in Colleges
and Universities

Edited by DWAYNE MACK,
ELWOOD D. WATSON *and*
MICHELLE MADSEN CAMACHO

McFarland & Company, Inc., Publishers
Jefferson, North Carolina, and London

LIBRARY OF CONGRESS CATALOGUING-IN-PUBLICATION DATA

Mentoring faculty of color : essays on professional development
and advancement in colleges and universities / edited by
Dwayne Mack, Elwood D. Watson and Michelle Madsen
Camacho.
    p.   cm.
    Includes bibliographical references and index.

    ISBN 978-0-7864-7048-8
    softcover : acid free paper ∞

    1. Universities and colleges— United States— Faculty.
2. Minority college teachers— United States.   3. College
teachers— Tenure — United States.   4. College teachers—
Professional relationships— United States.   5. Mentoring in
education — United States.   I. Mack, Dwayne, 1968 – editor of
compilation.
LB2331.72.M48 2013
378.1' 208996073 — dc23   2012034860

BRITISH LIBRARY CATALOGUING DATA ARE AVAILABLE

On the cover, clockwise from left:
Hemera Technologies/AbleStock.com/Thinkstock;
Polka Dot RF/Polka Dot/Thinkstock;
© 2013 Shutterstock;
Jupiterimages/Brand X Pictures/Thinkstock;
iStockphoto/Thinkstock;
Comstock/Comstock/Thinkstock;
Amos Morgan/Photodisc/Thinkstock;
Medioimages/Photodisc/Photodisc/Thinkstock;
Jupiterimages/Brand X Pictures/Thinkstock (*center*);
background Kim Steel/Photodisc/Thinkstock

Manufactured in the United States of America

McFarland & Company, Inc., Publishers
Box 611, Jefferson, North Carolina 28640
www.mcfarlandpub.com

Table of Contents

Table of Contents

Introduction
Faculty of Color in Higher Education

In spring of 2008, the University of Michigan became a flashpoint of tenure controversy. The institution had surprisingly denied tenure to assistant professor Andrea Smith, one of the most prolific Native American scholars in the nation. Michigan's decision sparked widespread outrage. Support from throughout the country for this beleaguered scholar-activist poured into Ann Arbor. Smith's tenure denial also captured national attention because in a sense the negative tenure decision represented a rejection of her Native American heritage, her feminist scholarship, and her antiviolence activism. While some might argue that Michigan's decision was not race related, many faculty of color will point out that higher education reflects a conservative "good old boy" sociopolitical vacuum. They might even reference former Harvard University president Lawrence Summers's disparaging comments in 2005 about the inability of women to earn tenure. His remarks reflected the rigid attitude of the academy's gatekeepers toward minority faculty.

Although we live in a society that is shifting globally, the academy is still hierarchically racialized. Compared to other professions, positions in higher education are traditionally white and segregated, reflective of a white hegemonic society. Because of the rigidity and relative reluctance to change, those in power and those that call the shots in the academy are committed to academia's dogma, which has been very conservative historically. Those in top administrative positions are those with the least amount of diversity of experience. While there have been increased recent calls for diversification of the professoriate, we have not seen dramatic increases in the number of faculty awarded tenure and promotion.

1

Faculty of color are keenly aware of the multiple obstacles on the road to full professorship. While there are informative books on the market such as K.A. Rockquemore and Tracey Laszloffy's *The Black Academic's Guide to Winning Tenure — Without Losing your Soul* (2008) and T. L. Cooper's *The Sista' Network: African-American Women Faculty Successfully Negotiating the Road to Tenure* (2006), there are no collections of essays offering personal reflections on the topic of tenure and promotion process from a diverse group of faculty of color. Although Peter Seldin's *The Teaching Professor: A Practical Guide to Improved Performance and Promotion/Tenure Decisions* (2010) provides excerpts from teaching portfolios, he fails to lend voice to faculty of color on the issues and concerns relative to them earning tenure and/or promotion. *Mentoring Faculty of Color* closely compares in target audience with Christine Stanley's *Faculty of Color: Teaching in Predominantly White Colleges and Universities* (2006). Her book serves as a platform for faculty of color to primarily discuss their teaching experiences at predominantly white institutions.

This collection of essays comes from underrepresented faculty who teach in somewhat racially and culturally homogenous campus environments. *Mentoring Faculty of Color* thus discusses both the tenure and promotion experiences of faculty of color and is not racial, ethnic, gender or discipline specific. For this reason faculty and administrators alike interested in the professional development and dilemmas of faculty of color in similar academic settings will find this study of great value.

Mentoring Faculty of Color provides inspiration for aspiring graduate students and tenure track faculty of color. By sharing reflections and strategies firsthand, faculty members are given the opportunity to reflect upon how they navigated the terrain of higher education. The Baby Boomer generation faculty is retiring at a rapid pace. Now, a number of Generation X (born between 1965 and 1979) are associate, and in some cases, full professors. Those on the latter end of this demographic are largely advanced assistant professors moving toward tenure. Within several years, we will see the same transformation among Millenials or Generation Y (those born between 1980 and 1992). This younger cohort of faculty is in search of guidance from academics that share similar racial, ethnic, and gender backgrounds.

Most of our contributors are at the associate professor stage of their careers. Some are full professors; all perspectives are rich, provocative and compelling. These experienced professionals connect to newly minted junior faculty by offering practical tenure and promotion advice. In its focus, this collection of fourteen essays remains multidisciplinary and inclusive. The book strives to be accessible and of great interest to the larger non-academic public open to learning about the tenure and promotion experiences of faculty of color. Contributors openly share with readers their ethnic and cultural identity, personal experiences as well as provide brief, yet specific examples of how they achieved tenure and/or promotion. The editors and the contributors understand the significance of setting professional benchmarks and assessing where they are in their respective disciplines. This understanding is why the dynamic collection of essays addresses the perspectives of faculty of color in regard to some of the following topics:

- Developing effective teaching and pedagogical strategies
- Developing a research and publishing agenda
- Dealing with realistic and unrealistic intersections of racialized content and academy expectations
- Creating underground networks with faculty of color
- Balancing service and teaching expectations
- Developing meaningful collegial relationships with junior and senior faculty
- Navigating the political waters at small, medium and large institutions
- Preparing the CV
- Balancing professional and personal responsibilities
- Gaining acceptance among colleagues as a parent
- Responding to subtle and not so subtle backlash against diversity and affirmative action efforts.
- Dealing with disrespectful, discriminatory, racist, sexist, religious prejudice, and xenophobic campus attitudes

Mentoring Faculty of Color appeals to faculty in the humanities, social sciences, hard and applied sciences. In essence, it transcends disciplinary boundaries. The book is of considerable interest and value to doctoral candidates of all races, ethnicities, and gender affiliations pursuing careers in academia. Moreover, related topics such as establishing good relationships with fellow faculty, department chairs, senior level administrative officials (deans, vice provosts, provosts), institution staff, and alumni are also discussed in detail. As faculty members who have been through this rigorous and demanding process this book is a valuable addition to the scholarship that exists on earning tenure and promotion.

Quantitative Dimensions

Historically, due to structural inequities in education, as well as persistent institutional racism and sexism in academia, women and minorities have had low representation in predominantly white colleges and universities. The current ethnic and gendered makeup of academic faculty in tenured and tenure-track positions suggests that, while some progress has been made, improvements in diversifying faculty are slow. While women of every ethnic group at the undergraduate level continue to outpace men in enrollments, faculty representation by gender and ethnicity does not mirror this growth. Thus, although equity in higher education has been a national priority since the civil rights movements of the 1960s and 1970s, diversity of faculty nationwide remains unacceptably poor.

Currently, on average, faculty members nationwide do not represent diversity by race/ethnicities in society, nor are they present in numbers to reflect student populations. For example, while blacks represent 12.6 percent of the U.S. population (Census, 2010) they represent only five percent of faculty. Latinos comprise 15.5 percent of the U.S. population (Census, 2010) and comprise less than four percent of faculty. White faculty comprise about 77 percent of all faculty, compared with 72.4 percent of the total population. Asian/Pacific Islanders hold about eight percent of faculty positions, higher than their share of the population, five percent (which is why they are not considered underrepresented in academia by some accounts). American Indian and Alaska Native persons represent 0.9 percent of the U.S. population (Census, 2010) and represent 0.4 percent of faculty (NCES, 2008). While the undergraduate student body is increasingly diversifying, the same is not reflective of the numbers of faculty of color in academia.

Overall, as reported by the Chronicle of Higher Education (September 2011), minority faculty (excluding Asians) represent between five percent and eight percent of all faculty in all institution-types (ranging from private non-profit four-year institutions to doctoral-granting public institutions). According to the most recent available data from the U.S. Department of Education's National Center for Education Statistics, doctoral-granting institutions (typically the institutions with the highest prestige) have the largest percentage of minority faculty members, as shown in Table 1. Looking at the data it is clear that higher education must continue to make strides in order for faculty to reflect student undergraduate populations.

Table 1: Faculty at Doctoral-Granting Institutions Only, by Race/Ethnicity

Total full-time faculty	White	Black	Hispanic	Asian	American Indian
309,466	229,598	12,857	10,375	31,786	1,138
	74.19%	4.15%	3.35%	10.27%	0.37%

Source: U.S. Department of Education, 2009 (adapted from the Chronicle of Higher Education, 2011). Excludes the following categories: "Race Unknown," "Non-resident Foreign," and "Two or More Races."

According to data collected in the 2010 Survey of Earned Doctorates, over the last 10 years, the percentage of doctorates earned by underrepresented faculty who are U.S. citizens/residents has been uneven. American Indian/Alaska Natives have lost ground and earned fewer Ph.D.s than 10 years ago (168 Ph.D.s awarded in 2000 compared with 122 in 2010). Among blacks there have been some gains (1,751 awarded in 2000 compared with 2,002 in 2010). Hispanics increased from 1,310 Ph.D.s in 2000 to 1,850 in 2010. Asians increased from 2,276 in 2000 to 2,828 in 2010. The number of Ph.D.s earned by whites remained fairly constant (in 2000 they earned 23,722 Ph.D.s and in 2010 they earned 23,508) (NSF, 2010). Women earned more than half of all doctorates in 2009, though these continue to be stratified by discipline, with women underrepresented in Engineering and some Physical Sciences (Chronicle of Higher Education, 2011).

The academic market for faculty positions is increasingly tightening nationally, and the competition for these positions continues to be fierce. Even in the current challenging academic market, despite some efforts made by colleges and universities to diversify faculty, white men continue to have a relative advantage over other faculty. As Table 2 indicates, white men outnumber all faculty in the highest ranking position of full professor. White men are still more successful at securing tenure track positions and advancing to tenure and promotion, evidenced by their overrepresentation at the highest ranks and relatively lower representation in untenured ranks of instructor/lecturer. This is telling because non-tenure track jobs are typically held by those who are unable to secure tenure-track ones. These data suggest there is no threat of diversity initiatives (or affirmative action) displacing white faculty. Women of all ethnic groups, by contrast, continue to be concentrated at the lower ranks, typically non–benefits-based positions characterized by low pay, and are often employed at less prestigious institutions. As Table 2 suggests, white women, black women, Latinas, and American Indian/Alaska Native women are comparatively overrepresented at the less stable positions of lecturer/instructor. Thus gender is salient in understanding academic rank. Women may be overrepresented in these posts because of institutional factors such as few mechanisms that support academic mothers/caregivers.

Thus, several racialized and gendered gaps remain in academia. As shown in Table 2, among faculty on tenure-track, at the untenured Assistant level, white men are represented at the highest percentage (41 percent) with white women following (33.6 percent). Asian men (8.7 percent) hold more positions at the Assistant level than Asian women (4.3 percent). Latino men hold a greater percentage (2.3 percent) at the Assistant level positions than their Latina counterparts (1.9 percent). Black women (representing 3.8 percent of all Assistant Professors) have a higher percentage of representation compared with black males (3.1 percent) in academia; however, there are higher numbers of black men at the Associate and Full ranks compared with black women.

The low numbers of faculty of color, and slow rates of change, have caused alarm among academic leaders. As noted in the journal *Peer Review*, published by the Association of American Colleges and Univer-

Table 2. Percent of Full-Time Faculty and Instructional Staff by Race/Ethnicity and Gender

	Professor (N=194,400)	Associate professor (N=149,600)	Assistant professor (N=158,100)	Instructor (N=82,700)	Lecturer (N=21,900)
White men	65.5	51.6	41.0	38.2	36.7
White women	20.3	28.4	33.6	41.2	43.9
Black men	2.6	3.1	3.1	3.2	2.9
Black women	1.1	2.4	3.8	4.4	3.0
Latinos	1.8	1.7	2.3	2.5	1.3
Latinas	0.8	1.3	1.9	2.3	3.8
Asian Pacific Island Men	5.7	7.0	8.7	3.1	2.4
Asian Pacific Island Women	1.1	2.9	4.3	3.1	4.0
American Indian/ Alaska Native men	0.8	1.0	0.7	0.9	1.3
American Indian/ Alaska Native women	0.4	0.5	0.6	1.1	0.7

Source: U.S. Department of Education, National Center for Education Statistics, 2003 National Study of Postsecondary Faculty (N=606,700)

sities, "At this rate of improvement, it will take more than 180 years for the black faculty percentage to reach parity with the black percentage of the U.S. population" (Jackson-Weaver et al., 2010, p.12). This quote suggests that, without targeted and strategic interventions, equity in higher education will be unattainable in our lifetime.

These data help shape our understandings of the climate within academia for faculty of color. Scholars are increasingly under pressure to publish abundantly in flagship refereed journals, present at professional conferences, teach well, mentor graduate students, contribute to conversations about innovative pedagogical advances, attend university functions with great flexibility, and commit selflessly to service work. Beyond these pressures, faculty of color often are drawn to, or called upon, by students of color in need of guidance; mentoring students of color is an additional unrewarded, and often invisible, task. Not only are faculty of color serving as advisors, often they are asked to work

7

together with admissions office, guest lecture during minority overnight recruitment efforts, serve on numerous "diversity" committees and job searches, and are often tapped by community organizations in need of research support or guest speakers.

Much of this service work by faculty of color goes unrecognized and is undervalued. For "tokenized" faculty of color, the devaluation of their work and the lack of a supportive academic community render the workplace isolating. In a recent article in *Peer Review*, the authors (all university administrators) reflect:

> Homogeneous academic departments and campuses that do not have organizations to support the needs of people of color can be great obstacles to faculty of color transitioning smoothly into a new setting... Given that most faculty members will spend many years at one institution, it is extremely important that they find themselves in an environment that nurtures their social needs [Jackson-Weaver et al., 2010, p.12].

In considering factors that affect the recruitment of the next generation of the professoriate, racial climate is one of the most prominent problems faced by minority faculty.

Notwithstanding, women of all ethnicities in science and engineering face tremendous isolation due to low numbers of representation. One review of 19 universities found that, across the board, faculty who are underrepresented report "the internal climate at their universities as more disrespectful, noncollegial, sexist, individualistic, competitive, nonsupportive, intolerant of diversity, and nonegalitarian" (Bilimoria, Joy, Liang, 2008, 432). This consistent array of negative perceptions found among underrepresented faculty in multiple contexts powerfully suggests that the social context shapes perceptions of inclusivity; this in turn can influence retention within academia. As a result, promotion to full professor can be elusive for faculty of color. Men are much more likely than women to become full professors. As Table 2 shows, the majority of white men in academia are tenured. Over 60 percent of all professors at the rank of full professor are white men; about 13.2 percent, total, are faculty of color at this rank, including men and women. What this tells us is the positions of greatest power, with decision-making control over the rank and tenure of others, are overwhelmingly held by a single group. This power translates into an ability to set the standards

[handwritten margin note: what are those organizations]

8

as to what constitutes excellence in teaching and research; it is against such standards that faculty of color are measured. For example, outputs in multidisciplinary journals are less prized; however, much work in ethnic studies is interdisciplinary and well suited for such journals. Scholarship and innovation in pedagogy is not valued the same as original research. Top journals tend to be formulaic and rigid, resulting in a very narrow range of authors who break through.

Failure to conform to these standards results in penalties against tenure and promotion. The issue of being a good "fit" for the university can also be raised with regard to collegiality. Inhabiting a marginal position allows for highlighting of differences, which are sometimes perceived negatively. Although "diversity" is a buzz word that is touted as important on college campuses, a hollow focus on this theme often fails to take into account the very real power relationships created by the overrepresentation of white men, and how these shape material outcomes for faculty of color.

Faculty of color find it hard to be mentored by capable senior faculty members who may not understand their unique needs. Finding one's niche within academia is arguably hard for all faculty, but it is especially taxing for faculty of color when they must also find community support for even mundane tasks (such as finding housing in a diversified neighborhood near the campus community, or finding hair styling salons or food markets that serve communities of color) others take for granted.

Beyond these basic community services, faculty of color must also redouble their efforts, namely:

- make their work visible
- establish the social importance and scientific merit of their work to defend their topics against ethnic and racial biases
- teach their peers about their research methods if they are not familiar with particular perspectives (such as oral histories of communities of color or autoethnography — methods that people of color in social sciences and humanities may be more inclined to adapt).

Faculty of color need acknowledgment and validation for the work they do. Another issue faculty of color experience is both overt

9

and indirect forms of racism. They encounter discomfort from students who might make assumptions of a lack of qualifications, as these students fail to see broader representation of faculty of color in the highest ranks of academia. Some faculty of color sense a lack of respect from students, causing fatigue and burnout for the faculty. Moreover, faculty of color need department chairs and deans who will take extra steps to provide protection from overwhelming service obligations, given the burden faculty of color face from overtaxation on committee work.

Finally, institutional measures can be established to create structures that validate work typically, but not always, performed by faculty of color. This includes acknowledging and rewarding, through the rank and tenure process, diverse perspectives in research, teaching and service; community engagement and public service; and mentoring and advising students of color and their organizations. Chairs, deans, and higher administrators need to participate in annual conferences and professional meetings addressing issues of mentoring faculty of color, to best understand the contemporary challenges faced by faculty of color. An infusion of education on these issues must saturate campus climates so all faculty can begin to recognize their own implicit biases, and work actively against them.

Faculty and Their Experiences

In this volume, tenured faculty of color discuss the various experiences they endured as they went through the tenure and promotion process at predominantly white institutions. From a holistic paradigm these academics utilize a number of approaches ranging from conceptual, empirical, and experimental by documenting the varied ways in which racism, sexism and other multiple "isms" affected their journeys in academia. Their stories also provide positive encounters as well as various mechanisms these competent scholars employed in an effort to combat the various forms of adversity each experienced at some point during the process.

These essays critique various issues including white male patriarchy, sexism, and the dilemmas of balancing academia with motherhood. Other essays examine, religious prejudice; hostile students and colleagues; the legitimacy of one's scholarship under constant attack, never being seen as "good enough" by some white peers; being directed to take on various administrative tasks; struggling to acculturate to the mores and customs of the dominant culture while frantically attempting to maintain your own cultural awareness; and reluctant mentoring from senior white and in some cases, fellow faculty of color, are just a few issues explored in these compelling stories. The diversity of these stories demonstrate varied experiences faculty of color often confront. Despite the ongoing presence of race there is no monolithic story representing all non-white faculty. That being said, their individual histories weave a concrete narrative of the potential perils often rumbling throughout the world of academia. The faculty represented in this collection come from public and private institutions. They are from small liberal arts colleges and research universities. Their academic disciplines are diverse and the regions they teach in vary as well. These factors contribute to a broad, inclusive and powerful narratives.

College and university administration can be a very taxing and meticulous experience regardless of race or gender. Nonetheless, faculty of color occupying such positions can carry additional burdens. They are under an unrelenting, invisible microscope. People question our competence and readily accuse of us of having biases. Moreover, they are watching to see if we will be partial to others who "look like you." "Is there a 'chip on your shoulder'?" "Will you be 'fair' to the majority group?" The challenges can be unique. Mark A. Pottinger and Tom Otieno provide very compelling stories of their experiences as administrators, one at a small private liberal arts college and the other in a university environment.

Women of color always have to be on guard for "Jane Crow," to quote the late feminist legal scholar Pauli Murray (1987). Jane Crow is the combination of racial and gender discrimination. Media images of women of color generate stereotypes that reproduce paternalism and biased ideologies in academia. Asian women have been depicted as either sensual and submissive or alluring and sinister. Latina women have largely been represented as animated, passionate, emotional, erotic and exotic. Black women are stereotyped as domineering, angry and confrontational. Indian women, including Muslim, have been seen as

11

mysterious, complex and out-of-sync with American values. Native American women are expected to be quiet and complicit. These stereotypes have infiltrated the halls of academia. Robin R. Means Coleman and Tasneem Khaleel have written very engaging narratives on their own experiences in dealing with, and navigating, negative attitudes of students who come to college filled with pre-conceived notions about women of color.

For many younger scholars who are on the tenure track, having good mentoring can be important or even crucial in obtaining such a goal. Strong guidance can also result in the difference between a stellar academic career as opposed to a lackluster one. The fact is for faculty of color the ability to find willing and or capable mentors (like many other issues), can be a challenge. A number of minority scholars are often in departments or institutions where they are one of very few or the only person of color. For other minority faculty this is compounded by the fact they reside in a region of the nation where the same faculty cohort are scarce or non-existent. Subsequently, the sort of research many faculty of color pursue is often seen as "suspect" or "lacking rigor" by many white, especially white male scholars. Because of these stark realities, Alyssa Garcia, Juliet McMullin, Judith Liu, and Toni Griego Jones have demonstrated in their passionate and detailed essays how they skillfully developed smart, comprehensive and common sense supportive strategies to help others successfully obtain tenure and promotion.

While having other faculty of color support groups can be an advantage for some, oftentimes situations may not make such a reality possible. One is often requested, if not pressured to acclimate to the mores, values and customs of the dominant culture. Your heritage must often take a back seat or become so obscured to the extent it does not make the majority group uncomfortable. The end result becomes a form of social isolation for many people. It is therefore imperative for faculty who live in areas where people of their ethnic group, culture or religion are minuscule or perhaps totally absent, find alternative strategies in an effort to maintain their cultural identity for themselves and their families. Dwayne Mack and Jacqueline B. Temple, Yer J. Thao, and Samuel D. Henry tell riveting stories of how they struggled with great determination to maintain their cultural identity and find a balance that is socially and psychologically important for their mental well being.

A number of women struggle with the balance of academia and motherhood. Many women who enter academia feel required to choose between the mommy track or the tenure track. Others who were determined to have children made efforts to delay childbearing until after they secured tenure and promotion or planned their pregnancies around summer months. Fortunately, a number of universities have become more sensitive and supportive to the needs and concerns of academic parents. Some colleges and universities have extended the tenure track for as long as 12 years, provided parent friendly policies, generous maternity leave and other accommodating options. Positive developments aside, women of color who are mothers on tenure track appointments still have a set of perceptions they often have to combat or effectively dispel. Michelle Madsen Camacho illuminates her experience as a Latina woman who encountered various reactions to her adventures in motherhood. Furthermore, she provides valuable advice and strategies for fellow women of color who have encountered similar experiences.

Successfully achieving tenure and promotion is a major accomplishment for many faculty. In fact it is the main prize in academia. The reality, however, is only half the journey has been accomplished. Attaining full professor is the highest rank one can earn in the academy. Obtaining the rank of full professor is another hurdle that must be planned for. Several years can transpire from the time of associate to full professor. Certain faculty and administrators who were crucial in one's journey to achieve tenure may have retired, left their positions and other circumstances may have resulted. Therefore, it is imperative that faculty who desire to reach this level attune themselves to meticulously acquainting themselves to the promotion process, focus intensely on research, navigating the issue of collegiality and cultivating the respect of influential people in academia. In his essay, Elwood D. Watson powerfully describes his eventful year as he successfully navigated various forms of racial animosity, personal vendettas, jealousy and to a lesser extent, ageism to earn his promotion to full professor.

For faculty of color it is important to have all the "i's" dotted and "t's" crossed. More often than not, faculty of color are not allowed the luxury of being subpar or even average educators. The public information we share about ourselves must be reliable and verifiable. Misrepresenting or falsifying our credentials can do serious damage. The old saying "you have to be twice as good" is a reality. One item all voting parties in the tenure and promotion process will view is a candidate's curriculum vitae (CV). This document will define who you are before and long after you earn tenure and promotion. Maintaining a professional looking and easy to read résumé can help a person advance their academic career. A poor or unkempt CV can stall your journey through the academy. In her insightful essay, Angela M. Nelson provides valuable suggestions on how to how to prepare, maintain, develop and revise the CV.

While many of us aspire to earn tenure and promotion and are pleased once we achieve it, the fact is not all of us are fortunate in obtaining this goal. The reasons for such an outcome often vary — ineffective teaching, lackluster research, hostile colleagues and other unexplained factors. The fact is no one can deny that failure to earn tenure and promotion can be a serious letdown for many scholars; however, it does not mean it is the end of the world. In her heartfelt and candid essay, Andrea Smith closes our book with the controversy surrounding her negative tenure decision. As a faculty of color who was able to professionally rebound, she provides as well as encourages innovative and psychological mechanisms for faculty who may experience such a fate.

REFERENCES

Aud, S., M. Fox, and K. A. Ramani. (2010). *Status and trends in the education of racial and ethnic groups* (NCES 2010–015). U.S. Department of Education, National Center for Education Statistics. Washington, DC: U.S. Government Printing Office.
Bilimoria, D., S. Joy, X. Liang. (2008). Breaking barriers and creating inclusiveness: Lessons of organizational transformation to advance women faculty in academic science and engineering. *Human Resource Management* 47, 423–441.
Census. (2010). U.S. Census Bureau. http://quickfacts.census.gov/qfd/states/00000.html Retrieved February 1, 2012.
Chronicle of Higher Education. (2011). http://chronicle.com/article/Sortable-Tables-Race-and/129099/ Retrieved February 10, 2012.
Cooper, T. L. (2006). The sista' network: African-american women faculty successfully negotiating the road to tenure. Bolton, MA: Anker.

Jackson-Weaver, K., E. B. Baker, M. C. Gillespie, C. G. R. Bellido, and A. W. Watts. (2010). Recruiting the next generation of the professoriate. *Peer Review, 12*(3), 11–14.

Murray, P. (1987). *Song in a weary throat: An American pilgrimage.* New York: Harper and Row.

National Science Foundation (NSF). (2010). Table 19. Doctorate recipients, by race/ethnicity and citizenship: 2000–10. Retrieved March 3, 2012, from http://www.nsf.gov/statistics/sed/pdf/tab19.pdf.

Rockquemore, K. A., and T. Laszloffy. (2008). *The black academic's guide to winning tenure — without losing your soul.* Boulder CO: Lynne Reiner.

Seldin, P. (2010). *The teaching professor: A practical guide to improved performance and promotion/tenure decisions.* Bolton, MA: Anker.

Stanley, C. A. (2006). *Faculty of color: Teaching in predominantly white colleges and universities.* Boston, MA: Anker.

Taylor, O., C. Apprey, G. Hill, L. McGrann, and W. Jianping. (2010). Diversifying the faculty. *Peer Review, 12*(3), 15–18.

Black Robe, White Collar

Achieving Tenure at a
Catholic Liberal Arts College
in New York City

MARK A. POTTINGER

"Let us remember that we are in the holy presence of God." These words by Jean-Baptiste de La Salle (1651–1719), which at first shocked me and now seem so commonplace, are spoken at every meeting of the faculty and students where I teach, at a Lasallian Christian Brothers College in New York City. This greeting reminds those assembled, either as an educator or as a student, that God is everywhere and watchful over all that we do. For most young faculty, the tenure process is felt in much the same way. One is mindful that the institution is always "present" in our academic lives and we must remember that if we desire "eternal life" at the institution (i.e., tenure), we must become like a servant to a master. We must serve on committees to enhance the institutional structure and makeup; conduct independent research for the betterment of the college's reputation; and teach the students with such profound and dynamic energy to allow departments to grow and prosper. This formula towards tenure at an academic institution — service, research, and teaching — is an age-old one and will not go away anytime soon owing to its quantitative and so-called objective potential for the tenure-selection committee.

What is telling in this process, however, is how it presumes equality of all its applicants, as if to say everyone at the institution has the

17

potential for tenure glory in spite of academic discipline, gender, color, or creed. As in my case, it did not adjust for the main factors that loomed large in influencing my tenure application, namely the difficulty of leading a small academic department filled entirely with part-time faculty, as well as my own minority status, a full-time black male professor and the only musicologist on campus. In the end these potential pitfalls for a young professor, new department administrator, scholar, and a person of color were turned into a powerful strength.

I entered Washington University in St. Louis in 1991 as a physics major and music minor. Early on in my undergraduate studies my major switched from physics to music, whereupon I began to seek a humanities education steeped in the liberal arts. In my second year, I received an Andrew W. Mellon Undergraduate Minority Fellowship (now known as the Mellon Mays Undergraduate Fellowship). The purpose of the fellowship was to award promising minority students with summer research grants and to offer a significant amount of student loan forgiveness. All of this was given by the foundation with the hope that if they were able to make it more economically feasible for minority men and women to choose a career in academia, then the overall goal to increase minority faculty at American colleges and universities is obtainable. The foundation only required that every Mellon scholar upon college graduation promise to seek a Ph.D. in the sciences or the humanities and then, simply enough, "change the world." Admittedly, as I began the fellowship my academic aspirations were only to earn my bachelor's degree and somehow to find a job.

In the summers of 1993 and 1994, with the help of the fellowship, I researched the 1842 and 1845 German concert tours of the French nineteenth-century composer Hector Berlioz (1803–1869). The faculty advisor of my summer research was one of the leading Berlioz scholars in the world. Moreover, my research reflected his interests, which happened to be the factor that came to define my academic career. In essence, my research goal was to compare Berlioz's account of his German travels as found in his published memoirs with newspaper articles, advertisements, and correspondences preserved in state libraries in Germany, Belgium, Austria, the Czech Republic, and Poland. The experience of retracing the French composer's life through his own words—a foreigner in a

18

foreign land — was one that had an immeasurable impression upon me, revealing the excitement and thrill of historical research. But, beyond that, the experience of finding my way was one that profoundly influenced how I saw myself.

It was not an easy task for a visible minority to travel through Eastern Europe soon after the fall of communism, let alone travel by one's self for eight weeks as a twenty-year-old who was relatively new to airplane and train travel. After getting over the shock of individuals staring at me without end, the constant shout of *Auslander* ("foreigner") by youths in Leipzig, or individuals spitting at my feet in Weimar as I passed them on the sidewalk, I learned to embrace my minority self in the face of constant marginalization and ridicule. Such an embrace presented me with an insight I still follow today, namely that I must not allow the external reality of what others see (i.e., prejudice) to define who I am, but to allow my ideas and my voice to articulate who I am and what others see in me.

After completing a master's degree in music at a British university, I returned to the United States in 1997 and entered the Ph.D. program in musicology at the Graduate Center of the City University of New York. While completing my course work, I was asked in the spring of 1999 to teach two sections of a general music history course as part of a humanities core at Manhattan College, my current institution. The two courses met three days a week, one at 8 AM and the other at 11 AM — not an easy schedule by any means. The teaching of two sections in music proved successful and I was invited by the dean to create and teach more courses. As those courses also proved successful, the dean then came to me with the charge of increasing "the presence of the arts on campus." The dean's invitation seemed relatively harmless enough, but the problem was that the college did not offer any degree programs in music, studio art, art history, or theater, nor did the college have any full-time faculty teaching in those areas. I would be completely starting from scratch.

At first I was a bit apprehensive as to whether I should accept the dean's proposal and attempt the building of an entire interdisciplinary fine arts program — including curricula, concerts, conferences, hiring of part-time faculty, etc. — when I myself was a graduate student with Mellon-inspired visions of working at a tier one-research university in an established musicology department. Sensing my possible refusal, the dean offered me a three-year visiting instructor position with the hope that if everything "all worked out" then I can use the three years of the visiting position toward a more permanent role at the college. In other words, if I indeed increased the presence of the arts on campus then the visiting position will open itself up to a tenure-track, assistant professor line. So often in American universities, people of color are forced to study issues of identity in order to carve out a space for themselves within a very non-diverse academic community, thus allowing one's minority status to be a position of authority the majority is forced to acknowledge. However, in my case, it was not only my minority self that had to be accommodated on the campus, as I was the only full-time black male instructor in the entire School of Arts, but my academic discipline as well.

I began the process of "increasing the presence of the arts" on campus by hiring part-time faculty to teach areas of music and art history that could be integrated with mainstream programs on campus, such as the "Psychology of Music" for psychology majors and "NYC Skyscraper" for engineering majors, or even courses of advanced study in such popular areas as "Renaissance Art," "History of Jazz," and "History of Rock and Roll." The new courses were heavily subscribed, which allowed me to convince the dean that instead of just offering the courses as electives to the general student population, we could also assemble the courses into minors. Although I was still writing my dissertation and teaching four courses per semester (4–4 schedule), the dean (as the de facto department chair) and I began the minor program in music and art history in 2004 and extended the program a year later to include digital media arts. Much to my surprise, a number of faculty at the college cautioned me that although such "service" to the institution was commendable, it could have a negative effect on my ability to achieve tenure at the college or even become a stumbling block in completing my dissertation. However, in the following year, after successfully defending my dissertation, and in spite of such warnings by my colleagues, I accepted the tenure-track assistant professor position in fall 2005 and officially became the chair of a bourgeoning fine arts department as the sole full-time instructor.

One would think that after starting minor programs, establishing college-wide performance ensembles, teaching inter-disciplinary courses, and participating in college-wide committees (mind you, all as a visiting instructor and graduate student), my new status as a Ph.D. holding assistant professor would allow me to bask in my success. I soon came to realize, however, that I was successful only in creating a space for my dual minority status to exist. In order to ensure a permanent place at the college I had to remain vigilant in showing the administration how my departmental programs and I are essential to the future growth of the college. If I was unsuccessful, both the programs I developed and the faculty I hired would no longer have an opportunity to develop at the college, nor would future students benefit from the critical understanding music and art bring to a college education. Thus, I needed to work not only on all three areas of my own tenure portfolio (i.e., teaching, service, and scholarship) but also lead a small department and its programs in order for both to survive past a five- to seven-year probationary period.

Since I did not have senior faculty within the department to guide me, I needed to find colleagues in other departments who served on the tenure and promotion committee and who could present me with insight on the overall process. Even though the faculty handbook defined the tenure and promotion process to be fair, balanced, and always in favor of the candidate, I learned from a number of senior faculty that the 16-member committee, which is made up of a diverse collection of faculty, deans, and administrators, often favored their own academic discipline when looking at a candidate's file. So in order for me to achieve tenure I needed to demystify not only my discipline and its accompanying methodology, theory, and application to individuals who had little knowledge of my field, but also my own specific work and research goals. To be clear, I did not begin with a game plan in terms of how to win tenure or influence people. In fact, I did not realize that what I was doing would truly ensure my success. I attempted only to teach well, pursue publication opportunities when they appeared, and be a friendly collegial presence on campus.

However, owing to the college's commitment to the principles of Catholic Lasallian education — the belief in the presence of God in all things and in all people, the respect for the dignity of all individuals, the veneration of social justice and the duty to serve the poor, and the acknowledgment that teaching is a ministry and it is a profound privilege to educate the young — I made sure all my activities honored those principles and found new ways to be expressed. Even if the everyday reality was not one of charity and respect, the college's mission nonetheless honors the minority voice (i.e., the poor, the disenfranchised, the lowly) and gives it a place of inclusivity. So, in order to achieve tenure, I needed to use the college's mission as my primary advocate of my service, teaching, and scholarship. And, in so doing, the college would come to see me as its own.

First, I asked various senior colleagues within the school of arts to sit in on my classes and observe my teaching. This served two goals: (1) it introduced foreign material to influential faculty, and (2) it showed how my teaching and the subject material were not too far removed from more mainstream areas of study at the college. Through this experience, I was invited by colleagues in other departments to share in symposia and college-wide talks, such as the role of music in defending one's civil rights or the influence of sound in our day-to-day world. Once again, this helped to create exposure for me on campus as well as prove to the rest of the college that I am a helpful colleague and I make myself available to others.

Second, I made it a goal to attend lunch at least twice a week in the faculty dining room, a table-service café with open seating. Through the opportunity of "breaking bread" with senior colleagues in other departments, they came to know me and I came to know them, in particular their frustrations with the administration, various departmental alliances, and personal prejudices. Owing to this exposure, individuals outside my department and the personal connections that developed, I was elected to college-wide committees. I happily accepted, of course, all of these invitations and sought to be a voice of fairness when making decisions on college-wide matters. One particular example stands out among many when during my second probationary year I was asked to serve as the chair of a judicial committee that was put together owing to a racially charged attack between an Irish-American student and three Hispanic students. The case was made even more volatile due to the fact it involved under-age drinking. In the end, I know I was asked to serve on the judicial committee because of my minority status, but, nonetheless, I used this opportunity to demonstrate to the college's lawyer, dean of students, senior faculty, and parents in attendance — that I am defined by the inclusive principles of the college and not by my own minority status. This particular case went far to put my name among others as the "go-to-person" for Lasallian-led advocacy of fairness and social justice across the campus.

Third, I became heavily involved in my local chapter of my academic society, where I served as a prominent voice within the meetings, either as a respondent to academic papers or as a presenter. This allowed me to set the agenda for future meetings of the local chapter, where I was able to host a meeting on my campus. The success of the one-day conference brought me further exposure on campus, especially after the publication of an article in the student newspaper, which, after being contacted by me, wrote a complimentary article on the growth of the department and its programs.

A fourth and final activity I pursued during my tenure process was to create curriculum beyond the service courses to the college, which would allow me to teach subjects in my scholarly area and thus create the potential for future conference papers and publications. Through our study abroad office, I was able to create an extremely successful course that met in Paris every two summers. The purpose of the course was to survey the musical activities both historic and current in Paris and Versailles in order to approach the broad issue of French identity. In Paris, the class conducted daily on-site lectures and discussions of the musical activities on the right and left banks of the Seine. Each class met in a specific location in the city where the location defined the musical style or aesthetic of a particular period of music history, from Ancient Gaul to present-day France. Following every on-site lecture, the students visited a museum where they were asked to find and photograph particular images relating to a musical activity of the period. For example, when we visited Sainte-Chapelle on Île de la Cité to discuss the crusade-defined world of Louis IX, the students were asked to photograph an image of men singing or playing a musical instrument on one of the many stained glass windows in this late Medieval reliquary. I have offered the course for four summers with great success. The course has created a deep intellectual relationship between the students and I, allowing the students to engage in my excitement for the material and make it their own. This proved rather advantageous as many of the students who took my study abroad course were part of other programs and so these students served as ambassadors of my teaching and material.

While in Paris I was also able to conduct research projects at Parisian libraries during my non-teaching days. It is often understood that summer research at particular libraries centrally defined in one's field discipline provides odd encounters with well-known colleagues in the field, who often introduce themselves (especially when they see a person of color in a place that requires special permission for access) and present opportunities for contribution to conferences and publications. This was the case for me during one particular summer, which, in the end, allowed me to increase both my list of publications and conference papers, as well as enlarge my list of recommendations writers. The experience of living, working, and researching in the very location of my research area was and remains tremendously satisfying to me, an experience that continually reminds me of my earlier time as an undergraduate. And like my undergraduate experience, I am able to gain life lessons that continue to encourage and sustain me during times of frustration with colleagues, school administrators, or even students.

All of these above activities were made possible by my minority status. Individuals on campus did not know my field or, for that matter, the intellectual presence of a person of color. I was able to educate them in how my discipline was academically defined and thus how individuals outside the field should understand it. My dual minority status gave me this opportunity, allowing me to embrace my marginality and to turn it into a space of respect and admiration.

I was awarded tenure in the fall of 2009. In conjunction with the start of my new status on campus, the fine arts department was granted new facilities and two new full-time hires in art history with more to come in the future. The department now has a major in art history, minors in music, art history, digital media, and theater. The possibility of a new major in music is likely as well. The success of the department and my own in achieving tenure were uniquely combined. The lesson learned from my "tenure story" is that for one who is marginally defined in scholarship or one's own racially defined self at an academic institution with little growth in these areas, then one has to connect with the college's mission in unique and broad ways in order for the maximum number of individuals to buy into what and who you are.

My reputation as a program builder, scholar, and supportive colleague are all due to this desire for collaboration with the college's mission, not just for collaboration sake as I have shown but for academic survival at a small liberal arts college. Fortunately, for me, owing to the nature of the institution, collaboration was seen as a cherished Catholic commodity, which allowed me to be accepted into that holy of holies for all junior faculty and to achieve a lasting space within the college and its programs.

REFERENCES

Ards, S., M. Brintnall, and M. Woodard. (1997, Spring). The road to tenure and beyond for African American political scientists. *The Journal of Negro Education, 66* (2), 159–171.

García, M., (Ed.) (2000). *Succeeding in an academic career: A guide for faculty of color.* Westport, CT: Greenwood.

Moody, J. (2000, May/June). Tenure and diversity: Some different voices. *Academe, 86* (3), 30–33.

Laura, P. (October 2001). Sex and race differences in faculty tenure and promotion. *Research in Higher Education, 42* (5), 541–567.

Tristano, R. (2009). *The idea of a Lasallian university: The relationship between the Lasallian charisma and the university.* Winona, MN: St. Mary's University Press.

Navigating the Tenure and Promotion Processes at Regional Comprehensive Universities

Challenges and Coping Strategies

Tom Otieno

The work of university faculty is typically viewed in terms of the three-fold functions of teaching, research/creative activity, and service. Those faculty navigating the tenure and promotion processes face several challenges as they seek to understand and meet expectations of their workload and the metrics, with all the nuances therein, for evaluating their productivity. Acclimatizing to the local culture of the new institution and region can also be taxing. The need to balance between the demands of the three parts of faculty work, and between their professional and personal lives, makes time management particularly challenging to all new faculty.

Faculty of color working in primarily white institutions, in particular, encounter challenges above and beyond those normally faced by all new faculty navigating the tenure and promotion processes. As documented in the literature (Chai et al., 2009; Stanley, 2006; Stein, 1994; Turner, González, and Wood, 2008), it is a reality that faculty of color and other underrepresented groups tend to be impacted differently by organizational structures and practices because of historical factors and societal practices. Institutional racism, prejudice, cultural insensitivity, marginalization, and devaluation of research interests are some factors that can have adverse impact on the performance of members of under-represented groups.

The purpose of this essay is three-fold. The first goal is to use personal experiences and those of colleagues to demonstrate that unique challenges in the tenure and promotion processes previously identified continue to plague faculty of color in institutions of higher education in the United States of America. The second and more important goal is to share with faculty of color pragmatic successful strategies for coping with some of the unique challenges they are likely to encounter as they traverse the tenure and promotion processes. Last but not least, the essay aims to sensitize the majority population about the unique challenges faced by faculty of color. The use of specific examples is intended to highlight some of the ways in which these challenges are manifested as some non-minority faculty and administrators may be inadvertently contributing to the environment that fosters these challenges.

I grew up in Kenya, a multiethnic African country, went to graduate school in Vancouver, a culturally diverse city in Canada, and now live in a small, predominantly white American city. I am, therefore, acutely aware that faculty of color do not represent a homogenous group. Rather, they represent multiple social and cultural identities. Yet, as the narratives of a very diverse group of faculty of color demonstrate, they experience similar challenges in predominantly white colleges and universities (Stanley, 2006).

The essay is based on my experiences as a faculty and administrator of color at a regional public comprehensive university of about 16,000 students, in which about 90 percent of the students and faculty are white. The dual role has provided me the opportunity to look at the situation from two unique perspectives. As a faculty member, I successfully applied for tenure and two promotions (assistant professor to associate professor to professor) within a space of eight years, and served on the promotion and tenure committees of two different academic departments (Department of Chemistry and Department of Physics and Astronomy), including chairing one of them for two years. As an associate dean, I chair the college promotion and tenure committee; I am responsible for the review and revision of the college promotion and tenure policies and

27

procedures; and I work closely with the sixteen academic departments in the College of Arts and Sciences as they develop and/or revise their promotion and tenure criteria and procedures. Furthermore, I advise faculty on best ways to prepare their promotion and tenure applications and departments on best practices in evaluating promotion and tenure applications.

Although institutions vary in how they rank, quantify, and assess faculty achievement, the general standards upon which tenure and promotion are awarded are teaching, research/creative activity, and service. This essay looks at each of these areas in turn. While the use of collegiality in personnel decisions in academia remains controversial (Weeks, 2006), it plays a significant role in the granting of tenure and promotion; hence a section on relationships with colleagues is also included.

Teaching

At regional comprehensive universities, teaching is usually considered the most important component of the three major areas of faculty responsibilities, and excellence in teaching is a prerequisite for tenure and promotion. If those who will make tenure decisions doubt an individual's ability to teach well, then that individual faces a serious challenge. Non-minority faculty or administrators, consciously or unconsciously, may, as a result of racial assumptions, doubt the ability of faculty of color to perform effectively in the classroom. Sensing or experiencing this attitude, the individual may respond by withdrawing. Such a response, however understandable, is doubly unfortunate, as it leads to marginalization within the department or university overall. Alternatively, feeling the pressure to "prove and over prove their presence and worth in the academy" (Stanley, 2006), faculty of color may over-apply themselves in select areas to the detriment of their performance in other areas, or experience increased occupational stress.

The following personal experience is an illustration of how doubt about my instructional ability was questioned by colleagues. At the time I was hired, my department had only one required method for assessing teaching effectiveness for tenure-track faculty. The method involved the administration of a standard student questionnaire with the knowledge of, and at a time chosen by, the instructor. My classes were evaluated as required. In addition, however, an extra evaluation was administered in one of my classes and in a rather unorthodox manner. The course had a laboratory component taught in open laboratory format, meaning students are allowed to attend the laboratory at any time it is open rather than being required to attend at a specific time. At any given time, the laboratory is occupied by students from lecture sections taught by different instructors. I learned the following semester that only students from my lecture section had been sought out during the open laboratory sessions and given a questionnaire to complete.

At that time, I was the first and only faculty of color to be hired on a tenure-track line in the department, and there was no precedent for this kind of secretive evaluation. Furthermore, even though we were two new faculty, my white colleague was not subjected to the same unorthodox evaluation. I could not help but feel that race was a factor in this expression of doubt on my instructional abilities. I wondered what would have happened had the student responses not been positive. I also wondered about some incidents that I had previously not dwelled on. During my first semester I had noticed, at least a couple of times, colleagues standing outside the lecture room as I taught. When I looked up, they walked away. Was this not a surreptitious attempt to verify if I, as a faculty of color, could indeed teach well?

Faculty of color are challenged not only by negative faculty assumptions, but also, sometimes, by their students who may question the faculty member's authority and credibility, or give unfounded, prejudice-based teaching evaluations (Stanley, 2006). Those who teach courses with multicultural or social justice themes appear to be particularly vulnerable. The following anecdote, as absurd as in may sound, is a good illustration of racial stereotyping. An African faculty member at my institution was headed to class to teach when he was approached by a student who had spilled something on the floor. Believing that the professor was a custodial staff, the student asked him to clean the spill. Although the professor was professionally dressed when the incident occurred, he began wearing suits to class. This incident explained to me, in part at least, why several of my African colleagues used to appear "overdressed" to me as they wore suits to work. While I always dressed professionally for the workplace, as an experimental chemist I could never imagine wearing a suit to work on a daily basis.

So what should you, as a faculty of color, do in order to overcome these challenges in the area of teaching? The first step is to acknowledge that prejudices will always exist instead of burying your head in the sand under the pretext that these issues do not exist at your institution. Accepting this reality will enable you to recognize and be better prepared to deal with prejudice when it occurs. Moreover, you may be able to use such situations as teachable moments to sensitize the perpetrators to the folly of their actions, or inaction, thereby contributing to a more positive campus climate for diversity. The next step is to strive to achieve excellence, as this will make it harder for those prejudiced against you to find excuses for undermining your advancement and also help combat negative stereotypes on competence and work ethics about your group. Start by understanding what your departmental colleagues consider essential elements of an effective teacher. Articulation of these institutional values can be obtained from the departmental promotion and tenure guidelines, departmental constitution and bylaws, and from conversations with colleagues. Some elements of the craft of teaching that are universally valued include being well-prepared for each class, demonstrating an excellent command of the subject matter, presenting material in a clear and organized fashion, using pedagogical methods appropriate for the discipline/course, having good classroom management practices, providing useful and timely feedback to students, being accessible to students, articulating expected student learning outcomes clearly in course syllabi, administering assignments and examinations that are clear and appropriate for the course in terms of relevance and rigor, and adopting fair methods of evaluating students' performance.

In addition to sound teaching practices, you should interact with students in a professional and respectful manner. How students perceive you will influence how they evaluate your professional performance which, in turn, will have a bearing on your career advancement. Some faculty of color not accustomed to student evaluations underestimate the power of student opinion of instruction, and the detrimental effect it can have on their careers. In my native country of Kenya, for instance, there is no formal process for students in public universities to evaluate their instructors, and the students rarely challenge the actions of their professors. Individuals who have studied or taught at such institutions often are surprised to find that there is accountability to students in universities and colleges in the United States of America. You should be ready to respond constructively to views on teaching gained from students and colleagues through student and peer evaluations. While this process may require adjusting the course work and teaching practices in order to help students achieve learning and meet course requirements, it does not mean that you have to lower academic standards.

Research/Creative Activity

Research/creative activity, the second area in which faculty are evaluated for the purposes of tenure and promotion, tends to offer the greatest challenge to faculty. Teaching and service generally involve other people and have well defined time-lines, clearly articulated expectations, and more institutional support. Research/creative activity, by contrast, is more of an individual endeavor where each faculty establishes his or her own pace, has more broadly stated expectations that leave room for subjectivity with regards to what is acceptable, and normally require more resources than can be provided by the university. Faculty of color face additional unique impediments in this area. First, faculty of color pursuing research agendas that benefit their communities (e.g. race, ethnicity, gender, diversity, culture, affirmative action, institutional climate) often find that such research is devalued in the promotion and tenure processes (Stanley, 2006).

As an example, a faculty of color at my institution (not in the College or Arts and Sciences) who had initiated a vibrant research program in South Africa found that continuing with that research upon relocating to our institution was not well received by some members of his department's evaluation committee (Otieno, 2012). The number of publications documented in his first two years of service was more than many people at the institution present for their promotion to associate professor and professor combined. This was an exceptional record, but the committee conducting his annual evaluation simply described his scholarly record as adequate and added that he needed to conduct research with a

Kentucky focus. The committee did not criticize his research methodology, the quality of his work, the contribution of the work to his discipline, and quality of his publication venues. The problem seemed to be that his research agenda focused on South Africa. Stein (1994) also describes a case in which an American Indian faculty was reportedly told that it would be impossible for him to do objective scientific research on his own people (Stein, 1994). He noted the irony of this situation since most research and publications about the non-minority populations are done by non-minorities.

At regional comprehensive universities it is common for there to be only one faculty of color in a department and only few in the entire university. Consequently, another challenge faced by faculty of color teaching at such institutions is that they do not necessarily have access to supportive informal networks, through which unwritten rules or common practices are shared. They may, thus, miss clues on important topics such as how to go about obtaining less well known internal resources for research/creative activity, and what really counts for promotion and tenure. Informal networks can lead to scholarly collaborations, or service on an editorial review board, or grant review panel. It is imperative for faculty of color to realize that not all significant promotion and tenure issues are spelled out in written institutional criteria. Therefore, the faculty should make every effort to understand the meaning of terminology in their field and the nuances that come to play in the interpretation of criteria. Any time a faculty member has questions about scholarship criteria, he or she should consult the department chair, members of the promotion and tenure committee, or other senior colleagues. How is research involving gender, race, or ethnicity viewed if it falls within one's discipline? If your research interests lie in any of these areas but there is ambiguity in the department regarding acceptability of such lines of inquiry and potential publication outlets, seek clarification in writing from the department chair. Are publications involving interdisciplinary work acceptable? Must the publication be in the subdiscipline in which one obtained his/her terminal degree, or could it be in another area based on teaching or service responsibilities?

There are additional questions that new faculty should ask to ensure that their research/creative activity record will be consistent with departmental criteria and practices. Must published work be peer-reviewed? Is publication in any peer-reviewed journal acceptable or is there some unwritten hierarchy that faculty are simply expected to know? Is an editorially reviewed publication acceptable when the criteria ask for a peer-reviewed publication? Boyer (1990) provided a framework for broadening the definition of research to include the scholarship of discovery, the scholarship of integration, the scholarship of application, and the scholarship of teaching. Is there a common and clear understanding in your department of what each Boyer category means? Does the department value all Boyer categories equally? How about co-authored publications versus single-author publications? Does the completion of work prior to joining the institution count if the publication occurs after joining the institution? Is a technical innovation, such as a patent, equivalent to a peer-reviewed publication? Is submission of grant proposals sufficient, or will only funded proposals be recognized? Do internal grants count? How much significance is given to professional conference presentations at local, state, regional, national or international levels?

Comparable questions apply to the performing and creative arts. For instance, is there any hierarchical order of performance, conducting, exhibition, production, or serving as curator with respect to outlet (on or off campus, local, state, regional, national, or international), venue type (museum, university, gallery, corporation, professional conference), number of participants (solo, two people, more than two people), or peer-review process (juried or non-juried, invited or non invited)? These questions may be useful to you in helping you develop your own list of concerns to take to your department chair, promotion and tenure committee, or dean. Having these conversations with your senior colleagues should provide you with a clearer understanding of what is being asked of you, but it will also help create candid, collegial relationships.

As already pointed out, faculty of color teaching at predominantly white institutions may lack supportive informal networks, leading to a feeling of personal and professional isolation. If you find yourself in such as environment, one way to build relationships and develop a support system is to participate in a formal junior faculty mentoring program if one is available (Otieno, Lutz, and Schoolmaster, 2010). In the absence of such a program, you should seek out a few individuals both within and outside your department, who may serve as informal mentors. For instance, you may have an individual within your discipline mentor you on issues pertaining to research, while someone else can offer advice on the nuts and bolts of the tenure and promotion processes. You should also reach out for support to other faculty of color who preceded you at the institution, as they may be better attuned to the challenges of being a minority faculty at a predominantly white institution. However, as in any situation where free advice is given, it is your responsibility to critically reflect upon the advice you get through these informal relationships. Some well-intentioned advice may not necessarily be in sync with your own aspirations.

For instance, several African colleagues counseled me, as the new kid on the block, that research was not particularly valued at my new institution and I should concentrate my efforts on teaching and service if I wanted to get tenure. The African faculty were relatively few (about 10) but it was difficult to not reflect upon a message consistently conveyed by the majority of those who preceded me at the institution. Nevertheless, I could not help but notice that the only one holding the rank of professor was a new faculty member who had been hired at that rank at the same time I was hired. All the others were assistant or associate professors, most of them still holding the ranks in which they were hired. My own ambitions went beyond tenure. I wanted to be promoted to the highest rank in the minimum time allowable by university policy. This ambition, coupled with my belief that each Ph.D. holder should first validate this research degree by demonstrating the ability to conduct independent research, led me to pursue an aggressive research agenda despite advice to the contrary by fellow African faculty. Consequently, I was able to achieve my goals of being tenured and promoted to the ranks of associate professor and professor in a space of eight years. Hence, while seeking advice from other faculty, including members of your own racial/ethnic community, it is imperative that you fully understand your departmental promotion and tenure criteria and begin to implement your research agenda as early as possible, certainly no later than the first summer of the first year of appointment.

Service

Service is the third dimension in which faculty are evaluated for the purposes of tenure and promotion. The unique impediment faculty of color have to contend with in this area is the hidden service workload often expected in the name of diversity. While these race-related service activities may benefit faculty of color by providing opportunities for achieving personal goals (Baez, 2000), they tend to be excessive, thereby becoming barriers to the pursuit of tenure and promotion. Examples include serving on an inordinate number of committees, appearing at several functions across campus, and serving as formal or informal advisor or mentor to students and other faculty of color. I give a couple of examples from my own experience. In the first incident, one spring semester I received a telephone call from the president's office, asking me to serve on a university-level committee. After agreeing to serve, I found out that the committee had already met several times and I was a late addition to its membership. The time scheduled for meetings conflicted with regularly scheduled meetings for all department chairs and deans in the College of Arts and Sciences. As such I was unable to participate much during that semester. However, I participated actively in the work of the committee during the summer months. Surprisingly, though, the following fall semester, no effort was made to find an alternative meeting time even though the co-chairs were aware of my scheduling conflict. I stopped serving on the committee.

In the second incident, I was surprised one day to receive candidate applications for the position of director of one of the units on campus. The search committee had advanced to the application review stage, and yet I had never been informed of my appointment to the committee. I politely expressed my displeasure to the leadership of the committee and declined to serve. Clearly, in both cases, my specific professional input was not really needed, and I was belatedly added to the committees, presumably, as a mere public relations exercise. Serving on these committees would have taken time away from other activities where my input was truly valued and appreciated or time that I needed for professional and personal growth.

So what can you, as a faculty of color, learn from these experiences in the service area? You will find yourself faced with additional service load above and beyond what is normally expected of faculty at your institution. By virtue of being a faculty of color, and likely only one of a handful at your institution, you will be asked to serve on a large number of committees or task forces and attend many events as your institution strives to demonstrate its embracing of diversity. You will be consulted on diversity issues by colleagues who assume that you must be an expert on diversity because of your ethnic background. You are likely to serve, formally or informally, as a mentor to students and other faculty of color.

Many of the added responsibilities in the name of diversity, while important, can take a lot of time and distract you from performing other duties that the reward system of the university recognizes more, thereby adversely impacting your progress toward tenure and promotion. One approach to addressing this issue is to strategize so that there is significant overlap between your research agenda and service activities, depending on your discipline. Another strategy is to negotiate with your department chair so that some of these race-related service activities are documented and recognized as part of your overall service load. This will allow you to cut down on your service activities in other areas. You should also be able to politely decline requests to participate in some service activities if you are already heavily committed to other service activities, or if the timing of a particular request is just not right. If you believe your placement on a committee is merely symbolic, you should feel free to ask why you were invited to join, or what *professional* vantage point you are expected to provide. This approach of judicious selectivity is better than accepting all manner of service activities and then developing a reputation of doing a poor job on service assignments, or jeopardizing your teaching effectiveness or productivity in the area of research/creative activity. Such matters, naturally, require astuteness, especially if the request comes from an administrator such as department chair, college dean, provost, or president.

In addition to service to the institution, many universities expect their faculty to be engaged in service to the community. In an academic context, service to the community refers to those activities where one draws on his or her professional expertise to benefit the local community such as community groups, business, education, or government. It is important for faculty of color interested in engaging in service activities in their own ethnic communities to find out if the department or institution has a position on that kind of service to avoid the risk of such activities not being recognized in tenure and promotion decisions. Ironically, faculty of color engaging in community service activities with the majority population also face the challenge of being unwelcome if the local community has not embraced diversity. This is particularly challenging if the nature of the discipline, such as social work, requires the faculty to work very closely with individual community members. It is important to inform your department chair if you are operating in such an environment so that your community service is evaluated in the proper context. These discussions regarding community service, like all other discussions with your senior colleagues, should come as early as possible, should be ongoing, and should not be delayed until the end of the probationary period.

You should start by reviewing criteria for service outlined in departmental promotion and tenure policy document and laying out strategies for meeting the requirements. As with research/creative activity, there are certain aspects of service expectations that will not be spelled out in institutional policy documents. Therefore, as a new hire, you need to seek some clarifications from the department chair or senior colleagues from the very beginning. Would mentoring students and/or faculty of color from within or outside your academic college count as institutional service? As an educator, would assisting local communities of color in their educational efforts be recognized as service to the community? Are all committees considered equal? Are services at the department, college and university levels given the same weight? Are new faculty expected to serve at all three institutional levels prior to tenure, or would serving at one or two levels suffice? How does one get on a college or university committee, especially as junior faculty? Are services to the profession and community valued to the same extent as institutional service? Must an activity be related to one's academic specialty to count as community service, or does coaching a local children's soccer team or working with the local Habitat for Humanity organization, for instance, count?

Relationships with Colleagues

Criteria for promotion and tenure at comprehensive universities are typically based primarily on the trilogy of teaching, research/creative activity, and service. However, the ability to interact and cooperate with colleagues and students has a significant influence on a faculty member's professional performance. While it has been acknowledged *vide supra* that one of the handicaps faculty of color face is lack of access to informal networks, it is imperative for you, as a member of this group, to cultivate interactions with your colleagues to the extent that they at least get to know you and your work, and to avoid being perceived as a lone ranger. The initial assessment of applications for tenure and promotion is undertaken by departmental colleagues, and their perception of how well you fit in the department and your contributions to the institution will set the tone of their report, which in turn will influence how other committees and administrators view your candidacy. Interactions with colleagues should not be limited to formal, work-related meetings.

Having informal interactions does not mean developing personal relationships with which you are uncomfortable and that extend beyond campus. Informal contacts can occur in faculty offices, in hallways, and over an occasional cup of coffee or lunch. These informal interactions are valuable for learning about unwritten rules and other common practices in the department and university that may have a bearing on one's tenure and promotion. These encounters may also be a way to reduce isolation and make the workplace a source of friendships as well as professional fulfillment.

To work collegially with peers and senior faculty includes being willing to listen to their assessments of our performance. Annual performance evaluations of non-tenured faculty provide the most useful means for untenured faculty to gauge their progress towards tenure and promotion. Therefore, you should review committee reports and department chair reports seriously and conscientiously address any concerns raised. If the process allows it, address the issues raised soon after receiving the evaluation report. If not, then offer clarifications, or explain what you have done to address perceived problems and needs, in subsequent rounds of evaluations. Failure to address concerns raised may lead to your being characterized as uncooperative and unresponsive to feedback, or unwilling to modify your work to the standards of your institution. Unfortunately prejudices will always exist but, as already pointed out (Otieno, 2012), not all unpleasant experiences between members of different groups are motivated by prejudice. Therefore, as a faculty of color, do not view all unfavorable evaluation reports as driven by racism, unless you have reasons. Since no one is perfect, take a critical look at the professional judgments of your peers before invoking prejudice. If your first reaction is to nonchalantly dismiss an evaluation report on the assumption that the evaluators are prejudiced against you, you run the risk of not taking any recommendations therein to heart, only to realize when it is too late that the recommendations were legitimate and could have made you a stronger teacher, scholar, or service contributor. Moreover, your peers may stop providing the honest feedback crucial for the success of junior faculty, for fear of being called racist.

Conclusion

Working towards tenure and promotion is a grueling process for most faculty. However, the playing field remains uneven and faculty of color encounter challenges above and beyond those normally faced by all new faculty. This essay makes use of my personal experiences and those of colleagues to highlight some of the challenges that are unique to faculty of color. The challenges include expression of doubt on their ability by colleagues, negative student attitudes and behavior due to misconceptions and stereotypes based on race, devaluation of research agenda, lack of access to supportive informal networks, and excessive service workload on diversity-related issues. This essay has offered pragmatic successful strategies for coping with these challenges. Some of the major pieces of advice arising from the discussion in the essay are listed below.

• Racism in academia exists and our very presence challenges it. Never forget who you are.
• Understand fully your departmental promotion and tenure criteria in the areas of teaching, research/creative activity, and service.

- Appreciate the fact that not all significant tenure and promotion issues are spelled out in written institutional criteria.
- Understand and practice what your departmental colleagues consider essential elements of an effective teacher.
- Interact with students in a professional and respectful manner and acknowledge the value and power of student opinion of instruction.
- Initiate and begin to implement your research/creative activity agenda expeditiously.
- Ascertain from your department chair the acceptability of research with race, ethnic, or non–Western regional focus.
- Participate in a formal junior faculty mentoring program and/or seek out successful and knowledgeable colleagues to serve as your informal mentors.
- Reach out for support to other faculty of color who preceded you at the institution.
- Negotiate with your department chair so that additional service activities that you are faced with because of your real or perceived expertise on diversity-related issues are recognized as part of your overall service workload.
- Exercise the option to decline, albeit cautiously, requests to participate in some service activities if your service load is already excessive by your department's standards or common practice.
- Cultivate interactions with your colleagues to the extent that they at least get to know you and your work.

REFERENCES

Baez, B. (2000). Race-related service and faculty of color: Conceptualizing critical agency in academe. *Higher Education, 39,* 363–391.

Boyer, E. L. (1990). *Scholarship reconsidered: Priorities of the professoriate.* Princeton, NJ: The Carnegie Foundation for the Advancement of Teaching.

Chai, H. H., J. L. Gilbert, K. Gunn, H. A. Harte, K. Ofori-Attah, and S. W. Soled (2009). Perspectives on facilitating minority faculty success in higher education. *Kentucky Journal of Excellence in College Teaching and Learning, 7,* 45–50.

Otieno, T. (2012). Making a difference in the daily routine. In S. Thompson (ed.), *Views from the frontline: Voices of conscience on college campuses* (59–79). Champaign, IL: Common Ground.

Otieno, T., P. M. Lutz, and F. A. Schoolmaster (2010). Enhancing recruitment, professional development and socialization of junior faculty through formal mentoring programs. *Metropolitan Universities Journal*, 21(2), 77–91.

Stanley, C. A. (2006). Coloring the academic landscape: Faculty of color breaking the silence in predominantly white colleges and universities. *American Educational Research Journal*, *43(4)*, 701–736.

Stein, W. J. (1994, Spring). The survival of American Indian faculty. *Thought and Action*, *10* (1), 101–113.

Turner, C. S. V., J. C. González, and J. L. Wood (2008). Faculty of color in academe: What 20 years of literature tells us. *Journal of Diversity in Higher Education*, *1*(3), 139–168.

Weeks, K. M. (2006). *Faculty evaluation and the law*. Nashville, TN: College Legal Information.

Were It Not for the Students, I Would Love to Teach!

How Women Can Manage Their Classrooms

Robin R. Means Coleman

I often joke with my colleagues that I would love to teach ... were it not for the students! Indeed, students can get in the way of my very best pedagogy because, it seems, some of them are unable to come to grips with the fact that I, as a black woman, am qualified to make a(n) (in)valuable contribution to their intellectual development.

Though, regrettably, often the only thing "black" in my classes is me and my box of Liquorice Altoids breath mints, some of my (predominantly white) students allow their prejudices to become a significant impediment to their learning. For example, the things that I say in the classroom are instantly "blackened" by my students without regard to content or context. To illustrate: In a recent class on audio technologies, I shared with my undergraduate students that country singer Patsy Cline had one of the purest, recordable voices I had ever heard. I recommended they listen to her smooth, graceful vocals through the "old technology" means of a record album and then compare its sound to digital technologies such as CDs or MP3 recordings. I even played the students a digital sound clip of Cline singing "I Fall to Pieces" to get the ball rolling. After class, a student angrily confronted me. She admonished me for discriminating against other racial groups and identities (read: whites and whiteness), as well as "forcing" (my) blackness upon students through the examples I offered in class. In this malcontent's mind, Cline, who is white, was assumed to be a black woman because black subjects are the only things that a black woman like myself can know and offer. As such, my exercise in active-learning—"having students engage in some activity that forces them to think about and comment on information presented," rather than have them simply listen to me lecture, was not successful for at least one member of my class due to resistance (Active Learning, 1993, p. 1). Her interpretation of my exercise was unfortunate as I really wanted everyone in the class to be able to not only reflect on the ideas I was presenting, but also to consider how they could draw upon their experiences to make use of such ideas as well.

Over the 19 years I have been teaching at the college-level, I have become accustomed to such ill informed, troubling "feedback" from students. I would be lying if I said such encounters were not unsettling for me. Still, I am no longer caught off guard by such moments, in part, because of the sheer, voluminous quantity of emails, anonymous notes, or remarks on my teaching evaluations over the years that variously state: "tell this professor this is not a black/feminist class" or "if I wanted a black/feminist class, I would have signed up for one."

Certainly, there are times when an instructor's identity leads students to make assumptions about how that instructor thinks or feels about certain subjects (e.g., affirmative action, human rights, blacks and/or women running for president, etc.). One way to mitigate such assumptions during classroom discussions is for the instructor to take on the role of discussion facilitator. In this role, we "can model constructive behavior in demonstrating how to unpack" issues and debates while also having students focus on their idea development rather than what our identities bring the bear (Guidelines, n.p.). To be clear, however, my observations are clear about when our identities (e.g., blackness and/or womanness) are brought to bear within discussion contexts where they really have no direct bearing. I am not arguing for invisibility.

Though I no longer give credence to such communiqués about the rejection of "black" or "feminist" classes outside of black or women's studies programs (and, just what is wrong with such a reach!?), making sense of such complaints' form and function are an important part of decreasing their sting. I have come to understand that what I am dealing

43

with is "co-cultural oppression," which describes interactions between dominant and nondominant group members while, too, acknowledging deviations in the definition of "dominant" and "nondominant." For example, a white male may concurrently be dominant (male, white) and nondominant (student, youthful) in a college classroom (Orbe, 1998a). A black female can simultaneously be dominant (teacher, older) and nondominant (female, black). Hence, we must account for the ways in which dominant and nondominant group members' status can shift in unexpected ways in communication situations, such as teaching and learning. For teachers, a failure to make sense of sources of resistance can result in one potentially finding herself being, as Orbe (1998b, p. 52) describes, "cautious, guarded, fearful, quiet, uncomfortable, not as outgoing, careful, and stifled" in the classroom.

In 2005, Clemencia Rodriguez, an International Communication Association (ICA) member and Associate Professor at the University of Oklahoma, challenged the ICA Women of Color Caucus to interrogate a type of "cultural war" waged against women in the academy by their students. I would like to extend Professor Rodriguez's call by attending to, in some detail, two lines of inquiry that she introduced and asked us to consider. They include:

• Did you once enjoy teaching, but now find yourself dragging your feet into the classroom?
• Are you receiving negative teaching evaluations in spite of your very best teaching efforts?

My goal is to come to this discussion from an instructor-centered perspective that privileges *our* professional and psychic survival. At times, my observations will border on the sardonic, however, I implore readers to recall the words of George Bernard Shaw (1918, n.p.): "all great truths begin as blasphemies."

Dragging My Feet, Reclaiming Joy

Encountering virulent resistance in the classroom based on one's identity certainly does not make for zeal-filled teaching. Some pedagogy literature charges the faculty member alone with working to disabuse students of their prejudices, rather than involving the students in their change as well. For example, one guide on hate and bias in the classroom tells the instructor to: (1) acknowledge the student's "issue," (2) tell the class there may be another view on the issue, (3) assess if the present is the appropriate time to fully engage the issue, (4) provide students with additional on-campus resources and groups that can shed additional light on the issue ... etc. (Guidelines, n.p.). To which I say, "good luck." The literature presumes two things: (1) that we are dealing with youngsters rather than young adults, and (2) that we are dealing with students' naiveté and ignorance rather than, at times, willful defiance.

On the first point, I believe that the college system tends to infantilize students. Admittedly, 18 years of age, the average age of a college freshman, is awfully young. However, in the "real world," by 18 years of age young adults have been afforded significant rights and responsibilities—the right to vote, the option of joining the military and going off to war, the opportunity to drive a car, own a home, and pay for utilities and daycare, the right to have an abortion without parental consent, the possibility of facing the death penalty, and the prospect of securing fulltime employment and even serving in supervisory roles, etc. I propose treating students like the young adults they would be in "the world." This means accepting that adults make mistakes, and that they should also be held responsible for the decisions that they make. Such a proposal is not offered lightly, for as Arnett (1994, p. 219) reminds, "most [American] college students consider themselves to be neither adolescent nor entirely adult," and that only 23 percent of the college students he surveyed thought of themselves as adults due to their slower, more gradual route to self-sufficiency. Interestingly, Arnett (1994, p. 223) found that one key indicator for adulthood for college students was an individualistic criterion —"*taking responsibility for my actions*"—something they found as an important benchmark for adulthood. Instructors, then, should move away from the permissiveness model of negotiation and reward when dealing with young adults. It sounds something like this: "Ok, interesting (classist, racist, sexist, etc.) perspective. Thank you for sharing. Now, let's discuss this more thoroughly. Are there others that would like to weigh in or take another stance?" This strategy sends the message that all discourse is equally valuable and valid, no matter how problematic. Instead, be prepared to, when appropriate, provide students with actual, scholarship-supported answers. This means telling students that they may have gotten something wrong (or right) based on research-informed and research-defined ontological and epistemological views. Be prepared to allow your students to hear your clearly articulated, wizened judgment on topics.

This brings me to the second point mentioned above about willful defiance. Be prepared that, no matter what strategy you adopt, some (young adult) students may willfully want you to be fearful, guarded, or stifled in your communication with them because of their own epistemologies about your sexuality, gender, race, or ethnicity, or because they reject the power education affords us. There is a wealth of literature that supports the notion of reestablishing your power in the classroom by making clear your professional capabilities while simultaneously demonstrating a caring for students' achievement; specifically instructors will benefit from "emphasizing credentials and qualifications on the first day of class and a commitment to helping students succeed" (Kardia and Wright, 2004, p. 5)

But what, you ask, of your resistance to the authoritarian model? Here, I am not talking about silencing a vibrant, dialogic exchange of scholarly ideas and debates. Rather, I am talking about controlling a classroom scenario that works to silence YOU; such a silencing is just as intolerable as that which silences students. Think of it this way: what are you teaching your students about; dominant and nondominant encounters when fear and discomfort takes hold of you in your own classroom?

Of Nannies and Mammies

There is another threat that women of color in the academy must be mindful of. That threat can come from within — that is, dare I say it, from others from within our identity groups. A few years ago, I attended a meeting for African American women in medical fields — physicians, high-ranking health care administrators, and health insurance company executives. The conversation among these approximately 150 women took an interesting turn. The women reported that they all had received multiple formal letters of complaint, and that the overwhelming majority of those letters came from other women. According to these women, their male colleagues, regardless of race received far fewer such letters, or none at all. Upon my return to my university,[1] I was asked to present at a workshop for faculty on integrating topics of racial and gender diversity into our teaching. During the discussion period of the workshop, I happened to mention what I had learned at the medical forum about the number of complaints levied at women. The female workshop attendees erupted agreement, sharing similar perplexing stories of what felt like the ultimate betrayal by "their own." They spoke of female students lodging complaints against them to their department chairs, deans, and even to other colleagues. Worse, these faculty members' colleagues at times did not know what to make of such, for example, "black-on-black" and/or "woman-on-woman" attacks.

At this workshop, one female faculty member confided that a female graduate student emailed a letter to the department chair complaining that the faculty member had not been available enough to the student's liking to offer a sympathetic ear. According to the workshop participant, the student's male faculty advisor was sexually harassing her; however the student never lodged a complaint against *him*. Rather, what angered the student was that she was not afforded the female faculty member's shoulder to cry on often enough as the student worked to figure out what to do. Sadly, such treatment of women faculty is not unusual. In a 2004 research report conducted at the University of Michigan by Kardia and Wright on the impact of instructors' racial and gendered identities during student encounters, 83 percent of students interviewed reported having different standards for female and male instructors, with students, across genders, making explicit their higher expectation for women (2004, p. 4). The researchers share this bit of qualitative data in their report (p. 4):

> I always have higher expectations for female instructors than male instructors. And, yeah, when they don't meet them it's a let down. And if it's a male instructor I tend to blow it off and say, "Well, that's typical...." I mean, I don't expect my male instructors to be as caring or concerned as I expect my female instructors to be. Whether that's good or a bad thing to be going on in my head, it's just a real thing. And it's pretty universal. (female student).

There are a variety of reasons students of all genders and hues hold women to a higher standard than male faculty. One reason may be the "nanny/mammy syndrome,"[2] where students expect, and often demand, a certain level of emotional attention from their female faculty. Nanny faculty are women who are expected to be nurturers for their students. Nanny faculty are assumed to care deeply about all parts of the lives of their students. Nanny faculty are to be ever ready to listen to stories about roommate, partner, familial, and financial aid problems. More, nannies are expected to have on hand a sack full of solutions and remedies—beginning with a box of tissues to wipe away students' tears.

Mammy faculty are women of color. They have all of the responsibilities of the nanny, such as offering students support and succor. However, there is the added expectation that mammy faculty will be wholly self-sacrificing on behalf of students. Mammies should have no other professional, familial, social, or civic obligations. Students drop by to see mammies at all hours of the day—without an appointment—for long talks. If mammies are involved in their own research and writing, they are expected to set it aside, saying "come in, come in! This can wait," while welcoming in a host of visiting students. Seemingly, if mammies do not like it, they should work from home, not in their offices. However, mammies should be forewarned, there is a risk to being out of the office, even for a lunch or bathroom break: students will protest loudly to all within earshot when their mammy faculty are even momentarily unavailable—"she's *never* here when I need her!"[3] What sets mammy faculty apart, however, is that they are also perceived to possess a rich depository of folksy wisdom —"child, if you believe it, you can achieve it!"

The purview of students' lives for nannies and mammies alike is usually that of the personal. Rarely are nannies or mammies seen as being expertly capable of advancing students' scholarly achievements. For this, students may choose male faculty advisors instead. A 2006 *The New York Times* article (Glatner, 2006) titled, "To: Professor@University.edu Subject: Why It's All About Me" implicates new technology in a sense of entitlement to faculty's time by students. However, a closer read of this article reveals an unexamined trend —"soft" academic requests are directed toward women, while men get quite the opposite.

48

In the article, five female and six male faculty are quoted. This piece on student entitlement unintentionally reveals that the demands upon women are largely service-oriented: asking for advice on what kind of notebook to purchase, seeking understanding for too much partying, and desiring empathy for familial obligations. Conversely, the demands upon male faculty by students are mostly about intellectual pursuits and class content: spend more time with those of us who comprehend the course material, spend more time on the readings, and summarize the main discussion points at the end of class. Quite simply, it is far easier for women to fail in their time- and emotionally-consuming nanny/ mammy roles, and thereby get those dreaded letters of complaint, than it is for men to fail in their professional roles, thereby avoiding students' scorn.

One solution is for women faculty to reorient themselves and their students about what their role is. Recently, a student from one of my classes came to my office to share with me a blow-by-blow account (pun intended) about fights he was having with his roommate. His roommate was also enrolled in my class. I worked hard to remind myself of what I do best — support this student's intellectual advancement. I am no student services expert. With this in mind, I first picked up the phone and set up an appointment for my student to talk to a student services counselor about the violence he was being subjected to at the hands of his roommate. I then engaged my student in how I could best support his performance in the classroom given that the presence of his roommate proved a distraction. We talked about moving his seat out of eyeshot of his roommate. We came up with strategies for him to participate in class discussion without him feeling that he might be later exposed to ridicule by his roommate and his roommate's friends. And, I found him a "study buddy" to review class materials with since his attention in class was so divided. We pursued these options until a student services counselor was able to meet with the young men, bring a halt to their conflict, and even eventually move the roommate to another class. In the end, I provided "professor" support, and student services division provided student counseling. Neither of us adopted a nanny/mammy role.

eBay and American Idol *Teaching Evaluations*

Very often our teaching portfolios are chock full of evidence that says that we take our teaching seriously. I build my teaching dossier by trying to attend two teaching-improvement related events each year. I then have a section on my vitae titled "Faculty Development" where I evidence the kind of "continuing education" I undertake to keep my teaching skills honed and my techniques cutting edge. For example, my vita includes entries such as: "Diversity Initiatives Workshop," "Learning Styles of Students," and "How to Become an OSCAR-winning Teacher." If I am at an institution that does not inquire about such activities, on my annual faculty activity report I append this information to show that I take my pedagogy quite seriously. More, on those occasions that I get a "if I wanted to take a black/feminist class" bad evaluation, being able to point to regular pedagogy training ensures that such criticisms do not stand alone, unanswered in my teaching record.

The value of student evaluations has long been debated. More recently, scholars have also questioned the usefulness of such an assessment for women and faculty of color. According to Merritt (2008) in her study "Bias, the Brain, and Student Evaluations of Teaching," women and racial minorities are plagued by lower quantitative evaluations than their male and/or white peers. She writes: "Students' contradictory and often hostile comments on evaluations of minority faculty, as well as their occasional direct references to gender or race, raise troubling questions about the role of bias in these assessments" (p. 236). Merritt is particularly concerned with how instructors' nonverbals—smiles, gestures, and other mannerisms—over knowledge, clarity, and other sound pedagogical tools—are assessed differently by students based on the instructors' race or gender. To put it plainly, social stereotypes can alter how and what students view as valuable about their instructors' pedagogy.

Qualitative reports, too, leave something to be desired in providing substantive feedback regarding teaching performance. For example, students earning an A grade in a course may love the instructor and the course. Students earning a failing grade will loath both. I call what I am seeing today as "EBay" or "American Idol" feedback. Happy students will write: "Great class!" or "Would take another class with this professor again." This differs little from my real EBay feedback: "Great buyer! A++++. Would deal with buyer again." Conversely, unhappy students tear a page from the American Idol/Simon Cowell book of "constructive criticism": "her last name is 'Means' and that is what she is," "I hate her," "she is a bitch," "she's a bitchy bitch," "she sucks."

I try to prompt more useful feedback from my students by doing two things. First, I conduct mid-semester evaluations in which students must offer qualitative feedback on not only my teaching, but also on *their role* in facilitating class success as well. I like to begin by telling the students, "now, this is very important to me. I wouldn't be using class time if it weren't. With this in mind, here are some of the kinds of feedback that has been less helpful to me, and ultimately to you." I then show them past examples: "A++++, great class," or "if I wanted to take a black studies class...," or "I hate her."

Since I began doing this, I have noted that students concede they have written such things about faculty in the past, and that they feel conscious-stricken once they see such remarks projected in a PowerPoint slide. With a sense of what not to write, I next address what students should attend to. For example, I ask students to discuss the strengths and weakness of my ability to advance their understanding and to facilitate discussion and debate, and I ask students to discuss their contributions to class discussion. I ask what they have learned from me and what I, and other students, have learned from them. Here, everyone in the class takes ownership of what it means to have a successful learning experience.[4] I then collect the responses and we discuss the feedback pertaining to my performance. This kind of evaluative process not only shows what form thoughtful, useful teacher evaluations should take, but it also reminds students of their role in fostering an educational environment.

Tough Choices While Keeping the Faith

Some faculty have, out of pure professional and psychic survival, opted to "water down" their course content, and even their "performance" in the classroom (i.e., their delivery and how they interact with students) to protect themselves from mediocre course evaluations and/or student complaints. Birnbaum (1999) in his article "A Survey of Faculty Opinions Concerning Student Evaluations of Teaching" observes that faculty he polled in the California State University system believed students' learning would improve with higher standards, but faculty are afraid to implement such changes as this would negatively impact their evaluations. As a result, Birnbaum (1999, p. 19) reports, "the majority [of faculty] judged that the current system of tenure and promotion discourages raising standards, encourages lowering of standards, and promotes 'watering down' of course content." To be sure, there are many strategies to evidence your exemplary pedagogy, such as peer evaluation and consultation/observation with your institution's teaching and learning center, alongside your student evaluations. Compromising your pedagogical ideals should never be one of them.

In the extreme, these are times when some students secretly record class sessions or collect reading lists of "radical" faculty to turn over to activist groups which create lists of "dangerous" members of the academy (Wilson, 2008). The tie that binds many of these "radical" and "dangerous" professors, the likes of Angela Davis, Derrick Bell, bell hooks, and Robert Jensen, who are viewed as indoctrinating students rather than educating them, is their advocacy for social justice on behalf of women in the academy.

Davis (2004, p. 95) warns against women, specifically black women, from reproducing racist forms of domination among themselves:

"She ain't black. She don't even look black." Or else, "She's too black. Listen to how she talks. She sounds more like a preacher than a scholar." Or, "Her work isn't really about black women. She's only interested in lesbians." Or, more generally, "She's not a real scholar."

Bell is famous for his sit-in protest against Harvard University's Law School, of which he was a tenured faculty member, for its failure to tenure black women. The attention Bell brought to the plight of women of all colors at Harvard was invaluable, even as it cost him his job.

hooks (1994) has been prolific in her attention to women's contribution to education. In her book _Teaching to Transgress,_ hooks not only calls for a progressive, transformative-centered pedagogy, but she argues that instructors must feel and be empowered, facilitated by a process of self-actualization, if they are to empower others.

Jensen has been writing about race, racism, white, and male privilege in the academy for over a decade. He famously pointed out in his now classic 1999 *Baltimore Sun* article, "More Thoughts on Why System of White Privilege Is Wrong," how much people wanted to talk about, and debate about, race and privilege with him, a white man. He does not shrink away from noting how even this attention to his ideas may work to reinscribe white privilege (p. C1):

> But probably the most important response I got was from non-white folks, predominantly African-Americans, who said something like this: "Of course there is white privilege. I've been pointing it out to my white friends and co-workers for years. Isn't funny that almost no one listens to me, but everyone takes notice when a white guy says it."

On one hand, sociologist Edward Shils (1997, p. 221) advances, "although academic freedom includes political freedom, it is nonetheless desirable that teachers should not expound their own political or moral preferences and values in their classes." On the other hand, educationalist Paulo Freire forwards, "if we accept education in this richer and more dynamic sense of acquiring a critical capacity and intervention in reality, we immediately know that there is no such thing as neutral education. All education has an intention, a goal, which can only be political.... So we find ourselves confronted with a clear option: to educate for liberation or to educate for domination" (Watkins, 1989, p. 101).

Indeed, female faculty must make some difficult professional choices about how they will secure what amounts to *social justice for themselves* in their own classrooms. Such a goal is not exclusively about what ideological, religious, or political part of the spectrum we inhabit. It is about restoring our love for teaching.

In the end, our mission should be to ensure that however we perform our best pedagogy, we do so with clarity, resolve, and importantly a critical consciousness that does not advance the continued domination, oppression, and silencing of women in their classrooms and in the academy.

NOTES

1. At the time I was on faculty at the University of Pittsburgh.

2. I wish to thank Ronald A. Lembo, a professor of sociology at Amherst College, for helping me conceptualize and name this experience.

3. Several years ago, when I was on the faculty at New York University, a student did exactly this when I took a quick bathroom break. I was not holding office hours on this day.

4. I wish to thank Rhonda Frederick, an associate professor of English at Boston College, for encouraging me to emphasize the notion of students' involvement and ownership of their learning on my midsemester, qualitative teaching evaluations.

REFERENCES

Active learning: Getting students to work and think in the classroom. (1993, Fall). *Speaking of Teaching: Stanford University Newsletter on Teaching*, 5 (1), 1–4.

Arnett, J. J. (1994). Are college students adults? Their conceptions of the transition to adulthood. *Journal of Adult Development*, 1, 213–224.

Birnbaum, M.H. (1999). A survey of faculty opinions concerning student evaluations of teaching. *The Senate Forum: A Publication of the Academic Senate of California State University, Fullerton*, 14, 19–22.

Davis, A. (2004). Black women and the academy. In J. Bobo, C. Hudley and C. Michel, (Eds.). *The Black Studies Reader* (p. 91–99). New York: Routledge.

Glatner, J. (2006, February 21). To: professor@university.edu subject: Why it's all about me. *The New York Times*. Retrieved February 21, 2006, from www.nytimes.com/2006/02/21/education/21professors.html.

Guidelines for discussion of racial conflict and the language of hate, bias, and discrimination (n.d.). *Center for Research on Learning and Teaching*. University of Michigan. Retrieved August 11, 2008, from www.crit.umich.edu/crittext/racialguidelinestext.html.

hooks, b. (1989). *Talking back: Thinking feminist, thinking black*. Cambridge, MA: South End.

hooks, b. (1994). *Teaching to transgress: Education as the practice of freedom*. New York: Routledge.

Jensen, R. (1999, July 4). More thoughts on why system of white privilege is wrong. *Baltimore Sun*, p. C1.

Kardia, D., and M. Wright (2004). Instructor identity: The impact of gender and race on faculty experiences with teaching. *CRLT Occasional Papers — University of Michigan*, 19, 2–8.

Merritt, D. (2008, Winter). Bias, the brain, and student evaluations of teaching. *St. Johns Law Review*, 82, 235–287.

Orbe, M. (1998a). *Constructing co-cultural theory: An explication of culture, power, and communication*. Sage: Thousand Oaks, CA.

Orbe, M. (1998, February). From the standpoint(s) of traditionally muted groups: Explicating a co-cultural communication theoretical model. *Communication Theory*, 8, 1–26.

Shaw, George Bernard (1918). Annajanska, the bolshevik empress (a one act play). Retrieved on January 27, 2012 from www.gutenberg.org.

Shils, E. (1997). Academic freedom. In E. Shils and P. Altback (eds.), *The order of learning: Essays on the contemporary university* (pp. 217–246). Piscataway, NJ: Transaction.

Wilson, R. (2008, July 23). Using new policy, students complain about classroom bias on 2 Pa. campuses. Retrieved July 23, 2008, from *The Chronicle of Higher Education*, chronicle.com/temp/email2.php?id=YvzcpDrjBrFng MwkCGrqPbqPFgjfFnsv.

A Bridge or a Wall

Struggles of a Pioneer Woman

Tasneem Khaleel

"The university is the site of a perfect storm of 21st century expectations and medieval bureaucracy, and the promotion-and-tenure process is the clashing point."

David Perlmutter, 2008

What an incredibly challenging yet rewarding journey it has been for me starting as an assistant professor of biology at then Eastern Montana College to my current position of dean of College of Arts and Sciences at what is now Montana State University Billings. It would have been an inconceivable thought 35 years ago considering the professional, academic, religious, cultural, and geographical isolation an Indian Muslim woman would feel in a state such as Montana (I thought people were being funny when they referred to it as the *redneck state*; but I did not know the meaning of redneck then!). Looking back, I wonder what influenced me most in my decision to stay in the department and in Montana: a moment of insanity, a sadistic streak, or simply the desire to make a difference.

Born, raised and educated in India, I prided myself for holding the first rank in the Master's program and being the first lady Ph. D. of Bangalore University. The ecstasy lasted until I stepped into the Indian job market, where my competition was male Hindu candidates with political pull. The consistent discrimination against my gender and my ethnic background disillusioned me and changed my thinking. I was looking for an escape from that environment.

Therefore, when my family arranged my marriage with someone who lived in the United States, the fantasy to have the best of both worlds, personal and professional, became real.

I perceived a university in the United States to be a place of communication and exchange of thought, a place of higher learning, a place that would embrace diversity, a place where I could grow intellectually, develop professionally, and practice my profession respectably. I wanted to be in an environment where I would be valued for my merits and not condemned for my identity. Little did I know that I would end up in Montana, an almost exclusively white state then (1976), with Native Americans representing the only color. The shade of my skin brought me closer to the Native American community members, some of whom, in their attempt to help me fit, called me "*another type of Indian.*" I was the only female in a department of all-male faculty and in an institution with a handful of female faculty, and the only Indian and a Muslim in the city of Billings.

Born, raised and educated in India, I had led a very sheltered life. Even though I was not a stereotypical Muslim woman wearing a scarf and walking ten feet behind a man, I was by no means "street smart." My approach to life was (and still is) idealistic. I believed in people and looked for the best in people. My friends often told me that a saintly attitude was only for saints and not humans.

In my naivety, I had envisioned the working environment to have the fairness of supervision of junior faculty, opportunities to collaborate, professional and personal interaction with peers that relied on intellectual vitality, and the interest of senior colleagues. I thought these were necessary to give me a sense of "fit" in the department. I expected to be treated fairly and equitably. Within the first few weeks, I realized none of my expectations were realistic. The institution and the department were at a transition for different reasons. The campus had been unionized only two or three years before my joining, and I was not the department's unanimous choice. Some of my male colleagues in the department openly commented that I fulfilled three affirmative action requirements. I laughed with them simply because I did not know what it meant.

Some faculty and students were willing to embrace the diversity I represented and others were in their own camp. I had never expected a conflicted environment. I realized I had to be better than the best in order to survive in the department. It was going to be a challenge to keep a positive attitude and stay focused, particularly with a two-year-old daughter to care for. I had moved to Montana with my daughter to start my career while my husband was finishing up the last six months of his veterinary medicine internship in Pennsylvania. I started to recall the quotes that I had grown up with: "When things get tough, the tough get going." "Heavy rains remind us of challenges in life. Never ask for a lighter rain. Just pray for a better umbrella." So I let the nerves of steel in me come out and began my journey praying for a better umbrella, knowing that some people will always throw stones in my path, and it depends on what I make with them, "a wall or a bridge." I also realized that it is not important to hold all the good cards in life. It is how well you play with the cards you hold.

I started my journey with examining the landscape of the department and observing the people in it. The Biology Department was small, made up of eight members, one of whom was the acting dean. The department chair had just been promoted to an associate professor, and I was told that he was not in favor of my appointment and to please him, my position, though advertised as tenure-track, was changed to fixed term after my arrival. This should have been enough for me to start looking for another job. But the tough in me prompted me to keep going.

During my first year, the department chair was denied tenure. He filed an appeal, and arbitration proceedings were set. He now turned to me for support. My first year, to say the least, was rocky, full of uncertainties and struggles to adjust and survive. My only companion was my determination to succeed and prove myself. Perseverance was not new to me. After all, I was the first woman Ph.D. in a field of study (botany) that was perceived to be male-oriented in India. My colleagues evaluated my performance in the second quarter of my employment. One of them (a self-proclaimed botanist) gave me an "F" on my knowledge of local flora, which, in his perception, I should have mastered by now despite the snow covered grounds (I arrived in Montana in September, and this evaluation was being done fifteen weeks later in January). Another faculty member reported that one student complained about my teaching, and therefore I did not deserve another contract; he was not willing to consider my evaluations from any of the other classes I taught. A third faculty member found me demanding too much discipline from students and lacking understanding of the "relaxed" classroom environment in America; a fourth expressed empathy, suggested I was going through culture shock, and was not sure if the department could afford the time for me to adjust. I was puzzled by these remarks. Don't all new faculty need time to adjust to a new environment, time to establish themselves and prove their worth? Does "relaxed classroom environment" mean students can throw soda cans across the classroom into the trash can or sit in the front row with their legs on the desk? Was I demanding too much discipline by asking those practices to stop in my classroom? Were these expectations of me alone because I was a foreign faculty woman? Would the expectations be the same of American faculty?

Subsequently, the position was re-advertised as a tenure-track line. I re-applied. By the time the search process was over, I had successfully completed the winter and spring quarters fighting the same battles and trying to adjust. Most of my colleagues, who were critical and skeptical, were willing to give me a second chance if I made it through the search. The search committee once again found me to be the most qualified candidate, and I was offered the position by the department chair, who was also the chair of the search committee. Before the offer could be put in writing, the former chair of the department informed me that it was not appropriate for the current chair to offer me the position without the approval of the department. All but the former chair were on the selection committee and I was left appalled and confused once again. Clearly, he was using the process to coerce me to leave. The acting dean sought a compromise, and I was offered the position on a fixed-term basis again. I could hear the echo, "It is not important to hold all the good cards in life. It is important how well you play the cards you hold." Do I continue in a fixed-term appointment for a second year or leave? Would I be building a "wall" if I stood up for my rights? The composition of the department was not likely to change, and the hostility of some faculty was obvious. I was the number-one choice in two national searches and was being victimized all over again. The proverbial "glass ceiling" was staring me in the face. I asked how this was different from India. Having the support of faculty on the search committee was comforting, but was it enough to combat the obvious hostility? I decided it was time to stand up for what was fair and right. After all, supporting wrong was no different from doing wrong. I decided to stand up for my rights by reminding the former department chair and the acting dean of the true meaning of affirmative action and equal opportunity. I was offered the tenure-track position with credit for prior years of service so that I could apply for tenure in the third year of my employment. The decision was met with skepticism and disdain by the former chair.

The former chair was an interesting personality. He was a skilled hunter and fisherman and took pride in the fact that he never bought meat, poultry or fish. Every word that came out of his mouth was gospel to his supporters. He had a cynical sense of humor, was short on compliments and was known to be a monotonous lecturer. Students perceived him as "the machoman" and feared his classes. Some students were retaking the same class for the third time! He did not believe in the union or in the colleagues who represented the union. Consequently, he was not going to be evaluated by any of them. All faculty who had been on campus for five years or longer were given tenure and rank advancement as part of the campus unionization. He was one of them. He openly mocked the union and the union representatives and ridiculed the process. The process being new, and the Collective Bargaining Agreement (CBA) being vague, no one really knew where the bar was to evaluate. There were no written departmental guidelines. The current department chair was the first one to have gone through the new tenure process in the department. The CBA allowed a faculty member to be promoted before tenure. The institution was primarily a teaching institution and to accommodate the existing faculty who came up for tenure, the CBA had allowed strength in two of the three areas, teaching and scholarship or teaching and service.

My second year of employment brought new revelations about my colleagues. The department chair was not successful in retaining his position through arbitration. He was now on a terminal contract. During the arbitration hearings, some of my tenured colleagues testified against granting tenure, and the former chair admitted that he lied in his promotion recommendation to keep the faculty line that the current chair held. I was shocked and wondered if I was setting myself up for failure. I wished they would make the expectations clear, what protocols to use and if there was a manual that I could follow. No one would even tell me how many copies of my tenure file I needed to make. I was not sure if it would be considered a weakness if I asked questions. Would I be confirming that I was vulnerable? Would it not be worse to not get tenure because I didn't ask? Who should I communicate with? The current chair, who was on a terminal contract, or the former chair, who was likely to claim back the chairmanship? The role of other colleagues in the department was marginalized. I realized that it was unrealistic of me to expect guidance on how to use my time, where to publish, or what project to do. None of them had gone through the process, and what I was thinking about was actually a three–five-year plan with appropriate time management and choices. I figured I had an active research agenda, an ambitious publication plan and plenty of time, ironically due to the lack of community in the department and in town. Therefore, with self-directed marching orders, I outlined a tenure preparation plan for myself recalling the conversation I had during my interview with the acting dean, who had said, "We need to strengthen the plant sciences and research; there are no pressures at this institution; the only pressure is the one you will exert on yourself; if you are self driven, you will do fine."

During the second year of my employment the former chair reclaimed the chairmanship. Calling his administrative style autocratic would be an understatement. He did not care to build consensus, communicate or consult with faculty in the department. Decisions about curriculum and other departmental matters were unilateral. The few conversations I had with him led me to believe he was a passive-aggressive person who loved to aggravate people and enjoyed watching them agonize. It was no secret that he hated plants, and I wondered if it was also extended to botanists since the faculty member who was denied tenure was a botanist. Being an animal physiologist, he did not understand the value of a herbarium in plant sciences. Therefore, my very first grant proposal to establish a regional herbarium by purchasing specimen cabinets and other furnishings and centralizing the plant collections from the U.S. Forest Department, Bureau of Land Management and Rocky Mountain College made no sense to him. My proposal sat on his desk for weeks until one day I told him bluntly that I was not using the money to furnish my living room and if he wanted to contribute to the demise of plant sciences, he could do so. I do not know if he had realized that he was testing my patience, had an objectivity attack, or maybe he did have a conscience after all; a copy of a glowing supporting letter to accompany the grant proposal showed up in my mailbox the next day. I wondered if I had made a "bridge" or "played my cards right" or simply showed him how "tough" I was.

I continued my research with no designated space and was the only one publishing in the department for a long time. This was the easiest one of my battles; the harder one was yet to come. I spoke Queen's English with an accent, and students had never been exposed to an accent. Some of them thought I spoke another language! Growing up in India with a British educational system, I was too formal for them. Students complained that I demanded too much discipline and taught at graduate level. I was not willing to compromise either of the above. Most of the students were older than me. My teaching evaluations in the first quarter were a blow to my ego. There was no teaching mentorship and I was unsure about how to improve given the cultural differences I encountered.

It is ironic that faculty hired to teach in colleges and universities seldom have formal training to teach. I had to figure out strategies on how to be a successful/master teacher in an American classroom of non-traditional students. I could have used some help. I wished some of the senior faculty would have invited me to their classes, but as they say, "if wishes were horses, beggars would ride!" Some of them sat in on my classes but had very little to say about my teaching style. They appeared impressed with my mastery of knowledge. As time passed, students were more accepting of me and my expectations. I also realized that most faculty and the students simply did not know how to deal with a foreigner. I knew about American culture, as most people from underdeveloped countries would, but they knew very little about Indians, Indian culture or Muslims. They thought all people from India were Hindu and followed a caste system.

The science building also housed the physical sciences. The faculty in physical sciences were collegial, helpful and professional. Most of them perceived the acting dean and the former chair to be arrogant, unprofessional, and lacking compassion and collegiality. One of them chaired the College Rank and Tenure Committee. By the time I rolled into my third year, the acting dean returned to the department as a faculty member. I prepared my tenure application with little help or guidance from anyone. I expected a review of my performance in each of the three areas with a recommendation for or against tenure. Instead, I received a piece of cardboard with a bull's eye with "tenure" written in it. I didn't know what to think. Were they trying to be funny and telling me that, hunters that they were, they had hunted for the right faculty member, or had my colleagues used my tenure application as an opportunity to mock and ridicule the process and insult the union members who were on the college rank and tenure committee? Do I laugh with them or be concerned? The chair of the College Rank and Tenure Committee did not think it was funny nor the portrayal of their hunter.

He was furious at the lack of professionalism and disrespect for the process. I was not aware if our Collective Bargaining Agreement had guidelines for independent evaluation by each evaluating body. I was justifiably nervous, as I had watched what happened to the colleague ahead of me in the process, and the policy is not always what happens in practice. I felt helpless. To their credit, the rank and tenure committee conducted an independent evaluation and recommended me for tenure, and so did the dean, the vice president and the president. The following year, I applied for promotion to associate professor. My colleagues once again made a mockery of the process. I was now sandwiched between my department colleagues, who were not willing to be professional, and the colleagues on the rank and tenure committee who were frustrated and humiliated by my departmental colleagues enough to forget that I was only a scapegoat. As a result, the department was reprimanded for not following the policies. Once again, I was at a loss.

I wondered, were my colleagues so conscious of my minority status that it gave them a false sense of security that my academic merits would get me past their attitudes, or didn't they care? Would a white faculty member be treated the same way? I had to wait for an answer until the newly hired white male faculty member in the department went up for tenure. This new faculty member was a fellow botanist who was a "no nonsense" guy. He put the department chair in his place soon after his first-year evaluation was done. The department chair had referred to his student evaluations scores as "adequate," and he argued they were "excellent." The department chair revised his letter to accommodate the faculty member. I couldn't help laughing, as my numerical scores in the first year which were much higher, were considered inadequate! Double standards were apparent. Should I have reminded the chair of what happened two years ago? Was the chair representing the whole department?

In a separate letter, the rank and tenure committee recommended me for promotion to associate professor which was upheld by the subsequent evaluators (dean, vice president and president). As time passed, my battles were not as fierce as before. I am not sure who was more sensitive to my being a woman, my colleagues or the department chair. Two years after I was tenured and promoted, my second daughter was born. Despite a difficult pregnancy, I had four manuscripts published/submitted during that year. My baby was born on the first day of spring. The only time I took off was the spring break when classes were not in session. Two of my colleagues commented, "You have understandably slowed down because of the new baby." I didn't know whether to laugh or get upset. Clearly, expectations were different for women than for men.

The department went through cycles of hostile environment alternating with somewhat tolerable environment consistent with other changes that were occurring on campus. It took a turn for the worse when one of the faculty members (the former acting dean) was not selected as dean. The campus graduated from "collective bargaining" to "collaborative bargaining." The Faculty Association replaced the American Association of University Professors (AAUP) on campus. The School of Arts and Sciences became the College of Arts and Sciences, and Eastern Montana College became Montana State University Billings. Despite the internal battles, I continued to publish, obtain grants, received several faculty excellence and merit awards, and served on numerous committees on campus. I became more visible on campus because of my work, dedication to the institution and devotion to students. The faculty in the college showed their respect by repeatedly electing me chair of the Travel Committee and the College Rank and Tenure Committee. I became known on the campus for my fairness, objectivity, analytical and problem solving skills, and consistency in process and practice.

It was not surprising when the Department of Foreign Languages asked me to chair their department when they had personnel problems. The lessons learned as a female foreign faculty member guided me through my tenure in that department. I was able to help them resolve their differences and reunite them as one functional department. In 1993, I was appointed to serve as the director of graduate studies and research, a position that brought me closer to other colleges in the university. In the meantime, the landscape of the department changed considerably. The biological and physical sciences departments merged into one department, and I was elected chair of the department. The former chair took early retirement. I wondered if it was to avoid working under a foreign woman or because he realized he was no longer supported. I was determined to make a difference in the lives of junior faculty in general and women in particular. As chair of the department, I believed in promoting a dialogue and encouraging junior faculty to ask questions about expectations and requirements. I also chaired the Department Rank and Tenure Committee during which time I was able to write and implement clear guidelines on expectations and procedures for tenure and promotion. Mentoring faculty in general and minority faculty in particular was very important to me.

Senior faculty who were never mentored often have a tendency to believe that the junior faculty should know what to do to earn tenure just as they did. I knew through experience, even with printed guidelines in a collective bargaining agreement or a faculty handbook, they "should know" rule does not always work for all. To assume a junior faculty member of color/other minority status knows what that means is absurd. I knew as department chair, I should not be giving divergent messages about expectations nor encouraging others in the department to do so.

Part of the tenure process, while it is based on the three traditional criteria of teaching, scholarship, and service, is also about being a valued colleague. While you can do a lot of things to prepare yourself, women in general and those of foreign origin or color need to find ways of making faculty, staff, and students feel comfortable with them. I recall an unmarried student who was pregnant deliberately avoiding me until I cornered her into talking to me. I realized she felt uncomfortable around me when she said, "I didn't know what you would think of me being pregnant and not married because unwedded mothers are condemned in your culture." I had to reassure her that I was not going to pass judgment on her character. During my first year of employment during warm weather, I wore the traditional Indian dress, the *sari*. One day a student commented, "Aren't you gutsy!" I didn't know what to make out of that comment. Am I showing courage by simply wearing something that I liked or did she think I did not fit in? Clearly, they had not been exposed to clothing worn in other countries. The news of my wearing *sari* made it to the media in Billings. A television reporter showed up in my office in the middle of January to interview me and was shocked to see me wearing Western clothes. He commented, "You switched on us, didn't you?" I realized they were expecting me to be wearing a sari even though there was a foot of snow on the ground and the temperature was ten below.

The 9/11 attack on the Twin towers in New York was an eye-opener for me and gave me a different perspective on how people think. I knew of religious discrimination in India but did not expect it in the United States. India gained independence from Britain in 1947, and Indians had to deal with the aftermaths of partition. Parts of India that were predominantly Muslim populated had become parts of the new country, Pakistan. There were people in India who believed all Muslims should have migrated to Pakistan. My family chose to stay in India, and I grew up with Hindu friends and a community that believed India was for Indians regardless of religion. After all, people now in Pakistan were in India before partition.

My oldest sister was married a few years after independence and lived in Pakistan with her husband. When the political relations between India and Pakistan worsened, communication between civilians in the two countries also stopped. My parents would become anxious at times when they did not hear from my sister. My Hindu professors helped us get through hard times by communicating through relatives who lived in London or the United States and who could call my sister and report on her welfare. I was grateful that I was part of that helpful community that believed in people.

The 9/11 attack on the Twin Towers in New York also brought new challenges to me. While the campus community was professional and supportive, there were people in the community who were not. I wasn't exempt from threatening telephone calls, hate mail, and hate writing in my driveway. Personal conversations from my home phone with my children mysteriously appeared in my voice mail on my office phone. It was "stones" thrown my way all over again, and I was faced with the same decision, whether to build a bridge by educating the community about my religion or a wall by ignoring it. Once again, the tough in me got going, and I spent countless hours in the community educating them about Islam and Muslims, most of which were received positively. As I reflect on 9/11 a decade later, I am staring at the typed hate mail I just received. I cannot help think that my struggle to build the bridge must continue.

Seven years ago, I was appointed dean of the largest college in the university, the College of Arts and Sciences. Among others, it was one of my goals to provide clear and consistent tenure guidelines to the faculty I hire. I made sure that I maintained consistent standards (performance threshold) and made recommendations based on the body of evidence. During the hiring process, I continue to ensure that department chairs meet with me and the candidate to be hired so that I can explain the criteria (what things are evaluated) and the process. The importance of giving constructive feedback regarding progress toward tenure cannot be overemphasized. I provide an analytical evaluation with feedback and encourage the departments to do so also. It is easy to give into a "don't ask–don't tell" academic culture, unfair and inconsistent policies and practices, and a sink or swim mentality when you have been a victim of those yourself. What is more difficult is to stand up against it!

Two years ago, the administration conducted a 360 evaluation of my performance as dean. It was most gratifying to read the positive comments and the respect my colleagues, particularly the faculty and staff, expressed. I felt elated that I did make a difference even though it may have been equivalent to a drop in the ocean; it was a difference for the good of the whole. Once again the ecstasy was short lived. I came across the Cornell University Faculty Work Life survey (Cornell University, 2006) which makes me question what has changed. According to this survey, women continue to find their departmental climates to be less collegial/more contentious, less cooperative/more competitive, less conciliatory/more aggressive, seeking individual advantage over collective good, and less cohesive/more fragmented. In addition, women feel less integrated/more isolated, less comfortable sharing their views in meetings, reluctant to raise concerns for fear of retribution, and less valued. Departmental climate is important to both male and female faculty members, but may have an even greater impact on improving job satisfaction and reducing intentions to quit for female faculty (Callister, 2006).

As I conclude my 36th year of employment in a still somewhat predominantly white male, institution, I am hopeful that the new challenges with generation X (Helms, 2010) may be different from what my generation endured. Tenure is still the goal, and mentoring matters, maybe more now than ever before (Trower, 2010). Together with a deeper sense of collegiality and community with broader networks, perhaps color, religion, nationality, and origin may become less important.

REFERENCES

Callister, R. R. (2006). The impact of gender and department climate on job satisfaction and intentions to quit for faculty in science and engineering fields. *Journal of Technology Transfer, 31*, 367–375.

Cornell University. (November 2006). *Understanding faculty satisfaction.* Cornell, N.Y.: *Cornell University Institutional Research and Planning.* Retrieved March 1, 2012, from http://www.ipr.cornell.edu/documents/1000369.pdf.

Helms, R. (2010). *New challenges, new priorities: The experience of generation x faculty.* Collaborative on Academic Careers in Higher Education Cambridge, MA: Harvard Graduate School of Education.

Perlmutter, D. (2008). Get another life. *Chronicle of Higher Education. 54*(27), C2.

Trower, C. (2010). A new generation of faculty: Similar core values in a different world. *Peer Review, 12*(3), 37–30.

Latina Faculty Narratives and the Challenges of Tenure
Identifying Strategies, Institutionalizing Accountability

Alyssa Garcia

In my early years as a Latina graduate student I was taken aback by and trying to make sense of the negative experiences I was confronting. I was unsure if I wanted to pursue a career in academia after obtaining my Ph.D. I questioned, "Would/could it get better? Would these negative experiences improve once I had my degree in hand?" In reality I knew little to nothing about the experiences of Latinas in the professoriate. With the goals of learning more about this topic to contextualize my then current experience as a Latina graduate student (as well as potential future career) I interviewed several Latina faculty at different institutions. This project culminated in the publication of "Counter-stories of Race and Gender: Situating Experiences of Latinas in the Academy" (Garcia, 2005). It documents and interrogates the differential oppressions in their lives, how race and gender, class stratify the educational and professional opportunities of these women. The article situates the pervasive exclusionary forces of racism/sexism at play that constrain and limit the lives and academic careers of Latina professors.

The first section of this essay will revisit the themes that the Latina faculty highlighted in my 2005 article: lack of mentoring/disparities, academic ethnocentrism, tokenism, and alienation/isolation. I then continue in the tradition of counter-storytelling, situating my own experiences, now as a tenure track professor, with these aforementioned issues. Almost ten years since the original project was conducted, the juxtaposition of my narrative with the original interviewees is a harsh reminder of the continuing reality of racism and sexism in the academy across generations, therefore highlighting the urgency to investigate the ways in which the dominant culture of academia identifies and treats faculty of color.[1] Having situated the experiences of Latina faculty, the next section theorizes perseverance by presenting a discussion of potential strategies faculty of color can utilize when confronting such challenges. As such, it hopes to open up a space for conversation across different generations to collaboratively discuss the process of tenure and promotion survival and proactively develop new approaches to our academic success. I then conclude with a discussion of individual agency and institutional accountability to argue for a broader definition of tenure and promotion success within a larger ideal of societal change that goes beyond the presence and perseverance of junior faculty of color in academia.

From Graduate Student to Tenure-Track Faculty

As a graduate student I was well versed and quite familiar with the themes of academic ethnocentrism, tokenism, alienation/isolation, and inequitable disparities that the Latina faculty interviewees highlighted, in addition to experiencing downright overt hostile racist and sexist incidents. Upon entering graduate school I was the youngest and only domestic student of color in my cohort, and one of two Latina/os graduate students in the department. I was told my research was "offensive"; I had problems securing research funding, I was told I "didn't know how to write"; I was accused of non-collegiality. Department administrators complained about the "Latino problem" and formal diversity related grievances were shrugged off via good intentions or relegated to culture of poverty-esque victim blaming (i.e., us students of color were at fault for "marginalizing ourselves").

Similar to the Latina faculty interviewees I individualized and internalized this failure and lack of belonging; I struggled to complete every semester on time. Today I reflect back on the trauma of what was graduate school, identifying some of the key arenas of support that enabled me to graduate. I found theoretical-intellectual inspiration and grounding outside of my ethnocentric discipline and department in Critical Race Theory and Ethnic-Latina/o Studies. I had an advisor/mentor of color that believed in me and provided unwavering support, and I mobilized with other politically-minded students of color in and outside my department.

Yet these resources and support mechanisms that kept me grounded and pushed me through graduate school were not necessarily available as I transitioned into a faculty position. When I first entered my tenure track position I was taken aback by the surprisingly welcoming and friendly environment of my department. "Was this possible? I wouldn't have to face blatant isms on daily basis? They liked me.... They really liked me?" I mistook the lack of individually directed overt hostility for equity. Yet I was quickly reminded of the more insidious and subtle institutional inequities that surfaced in discussions with the Latina interviews.

Academic Ethnocentrism

In their interviews all the Latina faculty confronted academic ethnocentrism, the ways in which the academy relies on a North American/Eurocentric canon as the frame of reference to make judgment on scholarship, which in turn makes faculty of color more susceptible to biased review (Tierney, 1996, p. 113). As Harrison notes, scholars are often socialized and/or pressured into upholding and transmitting frameworks that are determined by and conform to Western elitist interests (Harrison, 1991). This social hierarchy of knowledge indoctrinates paradigms of thought, defining the norms and criteria of academia. Thus faculty of color face particular challenges when their research falls under "nontraditional" areas or challenges mainstream approaches (Garcia, 2005, p. 264). Academic ethnocentrism undergirds the system of academic rewards and punishments; in turn discrediting and/or disqualifying anything deviating from the norm that does not integrate hegemonic ideals of knowledge construction (Aguirre, 2000, p. 70–72).

71

The Latina professors outlined the different ways in which academic ethnocentrism manifested in their careers and negatively affected their tenure reviews. They confronted the de-legitimization of their research and teaching topics/methodologies at every level of academic culture: publications, journals, disciplinary associations, professional networks, departmental resources, and funding entities (Turner et al., 2008). Turner et al. (2008) document how the undervaluation of research interests, approaches, and theoretical frameworks challenges the credentials and intellect of faculty of color in and outside the classroom. New approaches to research, teaching, and service that conflict with traditional approaches lead to poor evaluations and lack of publications (p. 149).

Frustrated, Dra. Castillo struggled to get her research on Latinos accepted into mainstream journals. Nevertheless it was always easier, "no problem," to get her studies based on whites published. Dra. Santana objected to the insulting way graduate students presumed she "didn't do theory." Studying race called into question her quality as a scholar (Griffin et al., 2011, p. 508). Grad students would unconsciously disparage her research and teaching. They would not take or value her courses because they "weren't as important," yet they would last minute expect her to be on their committees. Dra. Valencia lamented the ways in which academic ethnocentrism pigeonholes faculty of color. Given the nontraditional topics and more accessibly written nature of her research, her work faces harsher judgment (*ibid.*, p. 514) Deemed of lesser value, her contributions are questioned; there is always doubt about whether her research is "real." As Dra. Santana stated, "there wasn't a whole lot of respect for what I did. I don't even think people even know what I did or understood it" (Garcia, 2005, p. 265).

My early experiences as a tenure track faculty echoed the experiences of academic ethnocentrism the doctoras mentioned. In only a few semesters I was taken aback by the pattern of how and when graduate students would come to see me. Mostly students conducting research on Latina/os or in Latin America could stop by office hours only after they finished their course work. My expertise was clearly not valued by them; my work was only worthwhile in terms of logistics and area studies scholarship. They often apologized for not taking a course with me, but justified this curricular gap because they "didn't do race." Ironically, they would come to me asking for the necessary resources/bibliography before conducting research or request feedback for their M.A. thesis a week before their defense. At the departmental level race-related curricula was supported via lip service but never implemented. At curricula meetings when discussing the need to integrate racial topics or Third Wave feminism throughout our standard introductory course, I was informed that such material "was not central" and that students would "get it later in other classes." Yet, interestingly enough there were only a handful of race-based courses offered; the Latina studies class I was expected to teach had not been taught in three years, and was chronically under-enrolled since my arrival.

At the institutional level academic ethnocentrism was blatant and haunted my forthcoming tenure process. There was an explicit concern regarding the criteria and evaluation of my Latina/o studies related work. While my department encouraged my research, there was not a single senior Latina/o Studies scholar at the university with the expertise to thoroughly evaluate my work in a competent and effective manner. I would have to go on good faith that at the appropriate stage the tenure and promotion committee would select appropriate external reviewers. Meanwhile, the journals most suitable for publication of my Latina/o Studies based research were clearly not included on the list of "recommended" journals for tenure and promotion publication records. In addition, I was advised that my articles directly solicited by and published in bilingual or international venues "would not really count towards tenure."

Furthermore, there was little to no institutional support for Latina/o Studies on our campus. Our flailing "Initiative," which of course my hiring was integral to building, had scarce funding/resources. There was little impetus or stability for growth with the inconsistency of changing interim directors. The one Latina/o Studies course I was permitted to teach was consistently threatened to be cancelled each year due to under-enrollment. And the majority of courses listed for the Latina/o Studies minor could not be offered because there was not enough faculty to teach them, including the basic introductory course. Under the current system, Latina/o Studies was in essence set up to fail.

Tokenism and Cultural Taxation

The doctoras also highlighted the ironic double standard of academic ethnocentrism. Although their research/teaching on Latina/o Studies was de-legitimized, discredited, and devalued, an inherent contradiction existed in that they were assumed and/or pressured to teach/research such areas. The ways in which their identities become juxtaposed with their area of research (Garcia, 2005, p. 266) reinforced the hegemonic distinction between "real/unreal" scholarship. These assumptions not only limited their career choices, but also essentially doubled the amount of work they had to do. The doctoras pointed out this tokenization, and asserted how the identity and presence of faculty of color are co-opted and manipulated for departmental or University interests, which includes purporting the façade of diversity.

All of the doctoras contended with this commodification of race, ethnicity and gender in the academy, particularly in aspects of faculty service. Tierney (1996) elaborates on this issue of cultural taxation; good citizenship to the institution is tied to serving on committees and can place a heavy burden on faculty of color. The need for committees to fulfill a standard of diversity coupled with the larger institutional shortage of faculty of color, burdens them with greater expectations and responsibilities of service. Therefore faculty of color get "invited to everything" (Griffin and Reddick, 2011, p. 1044), especially those with joint appointments who are required to split their time between two departments. The doctoras also reflected on negotiating the contradictions of tokenization and cultural taxation. Dra. Santana confronted these issues on multiple fronts. For example students would relegate her to only knowing something about race, assuming she couldn't teach them anything else.

As a tenure-track faculty member, I quickly became familiar with the contradictions of tokenization and cultural taxation. I often had to extend my scheduled weekly office hours because there was a line of students inside and outside my office waiting to see me. Colleagues would comment how they would want to stop by and chat, but couldn't because my office was always bombarded with students. It was not uncommon that students who were not even in my classes would request my time.

Many were students of color coming to me not for academic guidance but serious psychological, economic, and cultural/race issues that clearly were not in my job description or training.

As a result of academic ethnocentrism and being one of the few Latina/o Studies professors at the university, each semester I bore the brunt of filling the gaps in our limited curricula with formal and informal independent study courses, especially with graduate students who had nowhere else to go to be trained in Latina/o or Latin American Studies. Given the lack of institutional support for the initiative (despite consistently strong student evaluations), I consistently faced anxiety that my Latina/o Studies course would be cancelled last minute due to under-enrollment. Each semester I was personally responsible for increasing enrollment, having to direct a substantial amount of time and energy into promoting my class by requesting cross-listings with other departments, posting flyers, sending email announcements, doing guest lectures in other courses, and attending student events (efforts that none of my white colleagues had to exert to ensure their classes would be taught). I was also dismayed when a department curricula taskforce suggested that my U.S. Latina/o course be conflated with a completely separate Latin American course to then be subsumed under a newly proposed Global Feminisms course.

I also came to understand the "biological determinism" the doctoras mentioned. At several committee meetings I was relegated to Latina/o Studies concerns and not considered or valued for my opinions on other areas or issues. On several occasions I was "volunteered" for service positions like Latina/o Studies activities coordinator and/or other Area Studies initiatives by senior colleagues (thus pressured to accept their requests). Yet, at the same time that this extra service was being demanded of me, fundraising resources to organize Latina/o or Latin American related events and inviting colleagues in these fields of study seemed to be the only ways I could engage in and remain abreast of these areas of scholarship given the void of such expertise on my campus.

Similar to the doctoras I was frustrated with this tokenization and the irony of how even though I was pressured into such commitments, they worked against my tenure and promotion process. Our department recently prioritized building our undergraduate program and I had received some accolades from a few colleagues for my successful efforts in doing so. Yet a senior colleague suggested I was non-collegial by not canceling office hours to attend department coffee hour talks. By the end of my first year review I was advised that for my future tenure and promotion process, despite their successes, I should limit mentoring and advising future independent study courses, as well as tightly restrict any additional service commitments or events. Although these service efforts significantly drew on my time and positively related to department goals/student retention, they were not professionally rewarded (cf. Griffin and Reddick, 2011, p. 1047). Work with students was not formally acknowledged, but instead viewed as disconnected from the academic realm (Valle, 2002, p. 165).

Confronting Isolation, Alienation, and Privilege

In the face of being pigeonholed into serving as advocates, faculty of color are often ostracized, discredited, dismissed, and/or considered to be acting out of self-interest (Jackson and Solis Jordan, 1999). The doctoras all identified with this, expressing how despite their qualifications they were often judged and/or relegated to the "emotional, angry, bitchy" Latina stereotype on a regular basis. As Dra. Valencia stated, "I had to just shut up and deal with it all the time" (Garcia, 2005, p. 268). In addition they pointed out the ironic ways in which their identities were put into question to disrupt their efforts and/or capacity to advocate for particular interests. Within traditional black/white racial paradigms, Latina/os weren't "real" minorities, especially if lighter skinned. These accusations of racial authenticity serve as an additional silencing mechanism.

The doctoras all recounted incidents of racial and sexual discrimination in the workplace, citing blatantly hostile incidents such as harassment. An interviewee in Griffin et al. (2011) well summarizes the consequence of this racism stating, "It's very clear that there is a significant segment of my department that in each step of the way would rather not [have] me here ... and they have made that very clear at this point" (2011, 511). The doctoras also emphasized the severe consequences of the

76

cumulative, more subtle acts of racism and sexism they experience on a daily basis. The work of Chester Pierce (cited in Solorzano, 1998) elaborates on the subtle forms in which racism manifests and the dramatic effects it has on the lives of people of color. He utilizes the term microaggressions to describe the automatic acts of disregard that stem from unconscious attitudes of superiority which often materialize in private interactions and conversations. Faculty of color experience these microaggressions in their daily lives, these incessant reminders that one does not belong or is considered inferior. These microaggressions are seldom recognized, investigated, or policed. Moreover, dealing with them and in the workplace environment of academia on a day-to-day basis is physically and emotionally taxing for faculty of color.

Like the doctoras I was quite familiar with the endless assault of microaggresions on a daily basis, always unsure if and how to respond to them. Like Dra. Valencia, I just had to suck it up and "deal with it all the time"; I never actually addressed them. In discussions with colleagues it was not uncommon to hear some unassuming racially insulting comment. I recall a colleague being surprised (on more than one occasion) when I responded that I didn't personally know "so and so," a feminist activist from Chile that she had met. Her comment, implied that all people of color know each other, collapsing any individuality or racial, cultural, ethnic diversity into an indistinguishable mass. Her question went beyond Othering; it conflated all difference and relegated it to the margins. Moreover, her assumption of U.S. Latina/o and Latin American interchangeability insinuated a foreign national belonging and in turn denial of my citizenship. In a similar vein, it was also not uncommon for unknown faculty who shared offices in the hallway to politely greet me by saying "hola" in the mailroom as if I didn't speak English.[2]

Unlike my white colleagues I also felt the immediate pressure of my teaching activities constantly being scrutinized and/or policed. Dra. Dominguez described the phenomena of "working under microscope" (Garcia, 2005, p. 270). In addition to the regularly scheduled semester teaching observations, senior colleagues would request to sit in on my classes as regular guests. Although uncomfortable with the proposition, I felt uneasy turning down senior colleagues and eventually was coerced into acquiescing. I had a graduate student whose advisor threatened to stop working with her unless she stopped working with me, dropped her Women's Studies concentration, and ceased to theoretically engage her work on Critical Race Theory.

Mentoring

Another important prominent theme in the doctora narratives is the explicit lack of mentoring throughout their career. They lamented the absence of other faculty of color and having no help or guidance along the way. These Latina professors expressed sentiments of feeling lost, having no clue, and being on their own. This frustration about having no support, counsel, or preparation in their academic process, lacking the cultural and material capital of white colleagues, made their transitions to the academy longer and more difficult. My experience echoed that of the Doctoras. While I was met with a general level of support and warmth in my department, I received no explicit guidance, did not understand the review process, and there were no senior people of color to engage for consultation. I was assigned two "mentors," who were very kind, but because our usual interactions were often limited to one social coffee meeting or meal each semester, they did not illuminate much information or advice about the tenure and promotion process. I, like the doctoras and most junior faculty of color, was desperate for mentoring.

Such a situation poses the following question, if this need for mentoring is so pervasive, then why are institutions so lacking in the structured implementation of mentoring programs? As Kerry Ann Rockquemore (2011) explains, there is a mystical understanding of what mentoring actually is. Administrators tend to assume that the best they can possibly do is randomly match senior and junior faculty, encourage them to have coffee and hope for the best.... Using the all-encompassing term "mentoring" focuses professors on connecting with a person instead of identifying their needs (Rockquemore, 2011).

Again, as faculty of color, we must assess the range of their individual needs, as well as identify multiple avenues for getting them met. It is also vital to ask without shame for the specific types of help that will meet your needs. Given the scale of needs, it is useful to pro-actively

78

cultivate an ongoing, diverse, and ever-expanding mentoring network internally and externally, as well as institutionally and personally. One should seek faculty members and resources within one's department, but also within the general campus. Faculty of color have successfully developed affiliations in other departments, centers, institutes and campus organizations across campus to foster intellectual development and make social connections with other faculty (Griffin et al., 2011, p. 512).

However, faculty of color also seek and maintain external academic networking and professional support beyond the confines of their campus (Griffin et al., 2011, p. 512). This can include former classmates, previous committee members, and interest group sections of professional associations. External support can also pertain to involvement in more institutionalized programs like the Mellon Mays or Ford Fellowships, one year postdoctoral positions, or summer programs like The Future of Minority Scholars Project. In addition one can request departmental or institutional membership in programs such as the National Center for Faculty Development and Diversity. And of course there is always the opportunity to establish new programs, initiatives, and organizations. Yet again, it is imperative for faculty of color to take the initiative to go beyond and not wait on formal institutional ties; construct your own personal networks. Build connections and do not burn potential bridges. Branch out when identifying potential allies; remember to select based on the color of one's politics/research, not the color of one's skin (or gender).

Brainstorming Strategies

The severity and implications of the challenges faculty of color face are not to be underestimated. However, identifying and documenting the experiences of faculty of color is not enough if there is not an ensuing conversation about how to overcome them personally *and* institutionally. In this light this section endeavors to present a dialogue about potential strategies for faculty of color when confronting the aforementioned difficulties. As Griffin et al. remind us, attrition and early withdrawal are not the lone responses; faculty of color respond through forms of behavioral/psychological departure and acts of critical agency (2011, p. 497).

Given the acute consequences of the ivory tower's racial/gender inequities/isms, one of the most important recommendations is to prioritize one's personal health and be proactive about self-care. When I entered graduate school, one of the best pieces of advice I received was "to find psych services as soon as I got to campus." Sadly, today I do not know of any female faculty of color who has not faced some level of physical or mental illness. A colleague once told me that women of color professors are four to five times more likely to develop significant health issues. As bell hooks noted, the public world of institutional learning is a site where the body had to be erased and go unnoticed. As academics we give in to the idea that we merely give ourselves over more fully to the mind. Yet, as hooks cautions, we must not engage in this mind/body split (hooks, 1994, pp. 191–193).

Our health needs to be *the* major priority. The reality is that only you are responsible for taking care of yourself. Therefore I stress the need to invest, as creatively as possible, in your own overall holistic well being, not only physical but also mental, emotional, intellectual, and spiritual. Be kind to yourself; allow positive self affirmation, and treat yourself to rewards. It is crucial to cultivate affirming practices that keep mind, body, and spirit in balance. Given the abrasive work environments being confronted, we cannot afford to lose sight of ourselves. I encourage those reading this book to be kind to yourself; embrace your strengths, but also recognize your limits and inherent humanity. If we demand consideration, protection and respect in the workplace, then that starts with how you treat yourself and your own mind.

Knowing that I clearly do not have all the answers, I asked some women of color faculty colleagues to share some of their personal strategies and thoughts on how to surmount some of the aforementioned obstacles. This is obviously not an end all or one-size-fits-all list, as faculty of color need to adapt such strategies to their individual circumstances and possibilities.

Academic Ethnocentrism

- Seek outside mentoring and external networks.
- Identify local senior colleagues who will reinforce the value of your

research and teaching so that you are not only person who has to defend it.

- Be confident in your abilities.... Do not let anyone or anything second guess your expertise. You were trained just like the rest of them and earned/deserve your place at the table. Academe cannot take back your Ph.D.
- Examine the critique being posed. Look at the suggestions, determine their validity, use your best judgment to evaluate if this commentary can be used productively, and proceed accordingly.
- In the classroom, push students academically to challenge their own views.
- Maintain communication with the head of your department to express your concerns about ethnocentric double standards.
- Attend conferences in your area of specialization. These provide opportunities to have conversations and interactions with people who share social, academic, political, and intellectual objectives beyond the limited perspectives of your own institution. Beyond similar interests these spaces also enable your work to be validated and get valuable feedback.
- Become involved in programming. Invite to campus the scholars you need to be in conversation with to give talks and workshops. This can provide opportunities to develop professional relationships, as well as validate your work by demonstrating there is a larger national conversation that you are participating in.

Cultural Taxation and Tokenization

To avoid spending too much time on service at the expense of your scholarship and teaching:

- Learn to say no! Find a balance between your ethics/values and what is expected from you to survive the tenure process
- Choose and Conserve: pick your incidental battles carefully and conserve your energy over time.
- Create a support network related to saying/practicing "No." Call upon senior mentors or junior peers to help you navigate your publish-service professional requirements. This "No" committee can help

81

keep you focused on your writing priorities and evaluate what service requests you should or should not entertain. This is vital to avoid that "used up and thrown away feeling" and empower your ability to actually say "No."

- Retroactively map out/quantify how you are spending your time. What percentage of your time is being devoted to research/writing, teaching, and service? Does your time spent actually match up with tenure priorities? If not adjust your time/tasks accordingly to reflect this.
- Be selective about the types of students you advise/work with (see first bullet point). You cannot take on every student who asks to work with you; it will hurt your productivity and what you are ultimately measured on.
- Be honest when addressing students.
  - Have conversations about what the tenure process is and/or how it institutionally positions faculty of color. If you are not comfortable speaking about your personal experiences, assign related readings or articles in class.
  - Let them know what they can expect from you. If you cannot serve their needs suggest another individual.
- Be realistic: You are one, only one, human being. You cannot do everything and it is not your sole responsibility to solve the world's problems. As a dear colleague reflected "Who died and made you Mama Africa?"
  - Speak to what you can when asked to speak for/about cultures that you do not identify with but that others connect you with (implying that you are imbued with or expected to have knowledge that you don't). You are not expected to know and advocate for everything.
  - Know campus resources and recognize your responsibilities/limitations. You are a professor (not a mother, brother, aunt, cousin, or friend to students). If you are not a financial aid officer, social worker, or psychologist, have a list of these contacts handy to directly refer students to appropriately trained assistance.

Isolation/Alienation

- Be in tune with your emotions and what you are feeling. Find a qualified therapist to talk to.

- Take breaks away from campus: Find and make time to connect with people and NOT discuss academic work/life to keep things in perspective. Do not feel guilty; breaks are necessary to surviving the long haul and maintain personal sanity/health.
  - Connect with and/or surround yourself with the people in your life that you love, whether that is via weekend travel, phone, or Skype. (Pets can count too!)
- Re-conceptualize institutional and personal identities. A known strategy has been for faculty to define themselves by relationships outside of academia, keeping personal and non-university life very separate (cf. Griffin et al., 2011, pp. 511–513).
- Identify allies on campus, in and beyond your department, who can be supportive of you work and serve as sounding boards, especially if you don't receive affirmation within your own program.
- Be proactive: Find one or two individuals that you can work with to keep you motivated; just having someone to work besides you makes a big difference. The benefits of a writing group, whether weekly or virtually, encourage productivity and accountability.
- Seek, find or create a community of like-minded and likely situated faculty of color. This may require "putting yourself out there" to meet other colleagues. Given that it is difficult for faculty of color to "be one's self" in predominantly white institutions, it is important to cultivate a space where one can have their guard down and feel they belong.

Confronting Privilege/Microaggressions

- (Ideally) identify at least one trustworthy senior colleague in whom you can confide and who will advocate for you. This ally can also serve as third party witness. If someone is not available in your department, then consider someone from the campus at large or externally.
- While draining, continue to keep these issues on people's radars. Consider subtle or more private ways to make people aware. While many people can be intentional and/or mean-spirited, many colleagues may be unaware that their statements/behaviors are inflammatory or problematic. A simple drop by the office or a social coffee chat can go a long way.

- Challenge labels/perceptions in a non-combative way by focusing/ highlighting the MANY POSITIVE things that those that are stereotyped actually contribute.
- Seek out empowering literature to channel your legitimate anger and frustration productively.
- Find a safe space to vent, whether through journaling or a non-academic person (therapy or like minded friends).
- Document and hold: Keep a detailed record of reflections on interactions, experiences, expectations that can be understood as oppressive, disrespectful or just odd (particularly if they pertain to race, gender, sexuality, language, culture, religion, etc). Keep such reflections/notes in suspension until processed and debrief with trusted colleague. Then, based on a number of variables/risks that YOU negotiate, decide to *act or archive.*
  - ◦ Creating a paper trail of incidents, emails, or documents may serve as evidence for present or future grievance procedures. While one incident may not seem worthy of addressing, they often add up. Faculty of color can sometimes demonstrate institutional racism/ sexism with this laundry list of microaggressions.

A Thought for Future Generations

I am often conflicted about giving advice to future generations who are entering graduate school or the professoriate. There is a struggle to find a balance of optimism and encouragement with a more grounded honest realism that can prepare them for the challenges that lie ahead. In this sense, I strongly agree with Dra. Santana when she states, "to avoid any sort of discussion about the difficulties ... is to misinform a subsequent generation about what it takes to be an academic" (Garcia, 2005, p. 272).

For me, it was humbling and empowering to hear and learn from the experiences of the Latina faculty interviews as I reflected on my own personal trajectory. At the same time these narratives are sobering and disheartening. They are a testimony to the embedded pervasiveness of racism/sexism in academia, the snail pace of institutional change, and how little has actually changed over the years. Like the doctoras before me, I felt like I barely made it through ... I just survived. Yet, I stand in gratitude when listening to these counter-stories of what we almost didn't survive, as well as those who eventually succumbed to adversity but carved out those paths that enable us to be where we are today.

For many previous generations of scholars the strategy (and advice I received) was "to get in and get out" and/or "suck it up." Silence could be and was an empowering and feasible survival tactic if inclusion was to be a realistic goal. Yet for me, that silence was debilitating, and inclusion clearly did not result in equality. Although the "isms" were constant, I was of a different generation within a different context, just as the experiences of future generations will be distinctive from mine. So while we can provide guidance and advice based on our past experiences to incoming cohorts, I recognize the goal is not merely to make future generations into replicas of us. The strategies outlined in this essay are merely to start an ongoing conversation about suggestions, not a handbook etched in stone.

In this light I encourage future generations of scholars of color to break from, not be limited to, and challenge the standard, traditional options of conforming, surviving, or leaving. Rather than posing the question as the late self described radical, black lesbian, feminist and poet Audre Lorde (1984) did, "Can the master's tools dismantle the master's house?," I look forward to witnessing incoming cohorts develop new tools, new strategies, and new houses. I hope that they can create their own uncompromising paths in academia, do so on their own (not anyone else's) terms, and construct safe spaces of belonging amidst a wider vision of equity and cultural citizenship. My hope is that these generations can create new ways of being scholars of color, to move beyond a framework of survival ... to thrive and flourish despite the constraints of racism/sexism in the academic world. I hope that they can empower themselves to be open to new choices and possibilities, to make academia inclusive and responsive to their goals and needs and not vice versa ... that they can stay true to themselves throughout the process and have a nourishing and transformative experience as a faculty of color.

NOTES

1. Counter-storytelling allows for an individual from an oppressed group to contextualize his/her experience, relieving a sense of isolation/internalized failure (Delgado, 1989).

2. As mentioned by the Doctoras I also experienced and observed the silencing of lighter skinned faculty of color with accusations of racial legitimacy based on a rigid black-white racial paradigm. For example, I witnessed an exchange at a departmental meeting when a senior white colleague attempted to racially discredit a junior African colleague by pointing at her skin and saying "but you're the same color as me."

REFERENCES

Aguirre, A. (2000). *Women and minority faculty in the academic workplace.* San Francisco: Jossey Bass.

Bell, D. (1980). Brown vs. Board of Education and the interest convergence dilemma. *Harvard Law Review*, (93), 518–533.

Chon, M. (1995). On the need for Asian American narratives in law: Ethnic specimens, native informants, storytelling, and silences. *UCLA Asian Pacific American Law Journal*, 3(4).

Delgado, R. (1989). Legal storytelling for oppositionists and others: A plea for narrative. *Michigan Law Review*, 87.

Flores, R. and R. Benmayor (eds.) (1998). Latino cultural citizenship: Claiming identity, space, and rights. Boston: Beacon.

Garcia, Alyssa. (2005). Counter stories of race and gender: Situating experiences of Latinas in the academy. *Latino Studies.*3, 261–273.

Griffin, K.A., M. J. Pifer, J. R. Humphrey, and A. M. Hazelwood (2011). (Re)defining departure: Exploring black professors' experiences with and responses to racism and racial climate. *American Journal of Education, 117*(4), 495–526.

Griffin, K. A., G. and R. J. Reddick (2011). Surveillance and sacrifice: Gender differences in the mentoring patterns of black professors at predominantly white research universities. *American Educational Research Journal, 48* (5), 1032–1057.

Harrison, F. (ed.). (1991). Decolonizing anthropology: Moving further toward an anthropology for liberation. Arlington: Association of Black Anthropologists–American Anthropological Association.

hooks, B. (1994). *Teaching to transgress: Education as the practice of freedom.* New York: Routledge.

Jackson, S., and J. S. Jordan (eds.). (1999). *I've got a story to tell: Identity and place in the academy.* New York: Peter Lang.

Lourde, G. A. (1984). Sister outsider: Essays and speeches. Berkeley, CA: Crossing.

Pierce, C. (1974) Psychiatric problems of the black minority. In S. Arieti (Ed.), *American Handbook of Psychiatry* (pp.512–523). New York: Basic.

Rockquemore, K. A. (3 October 2011). Mentoring 101: Let's stop talking about mentoring. *Inside Higher Education*. Retrievedfromhttp://app3.insidehighered.com/advice/mentoring/debut_of_new_column_on_mentoring.

Solorzano, D. (1998). Critical race theory, race and gender: Microaggressions and the experiences of Chicana and Chicano scholars. *Qualitative Studies in Education, 11*(1), 121–136.

Turner, C. S. V., J. C. Gonzalez, and J. L. Wood (2008). Faculty of color in academe: What 20 years of literature tells us. *Journal of Diversity in Higher Education, 1*(3), 139–168.

Turner, C. S. V., and S. L. Myers, Jr. (Eds). (2000). *Faculty of color in academe: Bittersweet success*. Boston: Allyn and Bacon.

Wood, J. L. (2008). Faculty of color in academe: What 20 years of literature tells us. *Journal of Diversity in Higher Education, 1* (3), 139–168.

Tierney, W. G. (1996). *Promotion and tenure: Community and socialization in academe*. Albany: State University of New York Press.

Trouillot, M. R. (1995). *Silencing the past: Power and the production of history*. Boston: Beacon.

Valle, M. E. (2002). Antiracist pedagogy and conceintization. In S. Sanchez-Casal and A. A. MacDonald (eds.), *Twenty first century feminist classrooms: Pedagogies of identity and difference* (pp. 155–174). New York: Palgrave Macmillan.

Beyond Toleration and Lip Service

Engaging Differences and Reflecting on Disciplinary Collaborations

JULIET MCMULLIN

Identifying the question

The choice of research topic in graduate school is one of those moments that direct your career for a number of years, if not through your whole academic life. A common assumption is that one should ask questions that move your discipline forward or that will sustain a rich and fruitful research agenda. While I agree that we should ask questions of such import, the assumption is promoted as if our questions must be decontextualized from who we are and how our colleagues and society construct us as individuals and as researchers. As I approached the moment when a research trajectory needed to be chosen I had two possible questions that revolved around issues of knowledge production and social inequality. While it seemed to me that these were straightforward research questions of theoretical and applied importance, their entanglement with identity politics and the creation of specific disciplinary identities and practices was anything but clear. It was a statement that was made to me at this crucial moment in my career that I often reflect on because it has come to symbolize a kind of intellectual and personal liminality. The framing of this mentor's advice demanded that I consider how my own personal history situates my career trajectory in particular ways, but also that I recognize the intersectionality of my experience I can shed light on how others use those categories to reframe my intentions for my career and their standards of disciplinary excellence.

The context in which my two possible research questions would be understood was, in part, driven by my own history as an ambiguously brown[1] woman. My father, who left my mother when I was two, was identified to me as part Hawaiian and part Filipino. That he was born and raised in Maui only solidified the notion that he was Hawaiian.[2] Following the pattern of identity that had been created in my father's heritage, my mother was part Texan and part Irish. Little did I know when I relayed these identity categories at the age of six that my construction of their identity as part ancestry and part geography was a better indicator of who they were than any categories of race that have been proffered. At the age of five my mother met and remarried the man who would raise me and my siblings into adulthood. Although he arrived from Mexico in his late teens his father (also of Mexican heritage) had come to the United States to work on the railways in the early 1900s. Thus, the color of my skin came from my father's ancestry, but the last name I used growing up came from my step-father's Mexican heritage. My mixed ancestry and own cultural history resulted in my being categorized as any brown ethnicity people wanted to claim for me. As I was growing up ancestral clarity was never achieved because my mother desired to raise my siblings and me as white Americans, while also maintaining the romanticized brownness of our fathers.

It is in both the ambiguity of brown and the confusion of heritage that one statement was made that resulted in my refusal to release the ambiguity and to understand why I intellectually would not define myself in the disciplinary categories provided to me. During my second year of graduate school I approached one of my mentors and told him of my two thoughts for a dissertation project. The first thought would be to continue working on issues related to cancer inequalities. At the time I was working as a research assistant that was co-led by my primary mentor (an anthropologist) and a physician. This project was funded by the National Cancer Institute and examined the knowledge, practices, and risks surrounding breast and cervical cancer among Latinas and physicians in Southern California. The second thought I had was to examine intersections of the production of health and the Native Hawaiian sovereignty movement. Granted my chosen field of study is a discipline that has a long history of constructing the exotic, but I was still shocked when this secondary mentor told me that I should not pursue a research career in the area of cancer but rather work in a geographical area that was more "exotic." He remarked "you don't want to become known as the cancer lady." Reflecting back on this statement, I realize that much more was being said about how to identify an acceptable research topic as well as how research was supposed to be conducted. And yet, the decision about what topic to choose was embedded with the simple and horrifying exotification of me and my idea of conducting fieldwork with Native Hawaiians.

The explicit issue for this mentor was that cancer, as a research topic, was too narrowly focused to maintain a career in anthropology. Focusing on Native Hawaiians as the topic, however, would invite all sorts of questions about other cultural ways of being human. Specifically, "exotic" ways of being human. I was being asked to simultaneously embody part of a dominant educated society while denying the representation of the brownness of my skin. The salvation of the brown woman by the white man would take place in his implicit concerns. These concerns focused on a need to differentiate my own work from the work of my primary advisor. I needed to demonstrate where my own intellectual self started and where those of my primary mentor ended. It is not that I really disagree with this thought, because it is important that scholars show intellectual independence. In this moment, however, it was also clear that for me to be a successful scholar my discipline demanded a demonstration of sole/single/individual scholarship. I needed to be the sole researcher in my project and have single authored refereed publications. I must note here that this is somewhat different from the biological and natural sciences that also demand a demonstration of independent scholarship that is that the scholar is capable of developing, implementing, analyzing, and reporting on their chosen research agenda. Being an independent researcher, however, does not mean that the project is done alone. Research teams are organized and individuals with required areas of expertise are brought together to share knowledge, discuss avenues of inquiry, and to move the knowledge of a discipline forward. As a scholar becomes an independent researcher she moves from playing a supporting role in the conduct and publication of the research into a leading role. Had I not been employed by a interdisciplinary research project as a graduate student, it is unclear to me that I would have known that collective effort in research and publication was an option to the sole effort that I was being encouraged to pursue. Both frameworks have their strengths and pitfalls as they are used in the creation and evaluation of our careers. Their meaning however, must not be taken for granted as simple disciplinary preferences, but rather as specific ways of creating exclusionary categories that are occasionally wielded to derail minority scholars from achieving excellence in their careers.

The issue of collaborative research in my own subfield is particularly problematic because its scholarship exists exactly in those spaces from which I was dissuaded. When anthropologists talk about collaborative research, we are often talking about collaboration with the communities with whom we work. Rarely do we talk about collaboration with other disciplines within the academy or including the names of those who have contributed to a publication as co-authors. When we do broach the topic of interdisciplinary work our stories are fraught with fears of becoming handmaidens to the goals of other disciplines, and incidents of incommensurability and cultural tokenism (Scheper-Hughes, 1990). Medical anthropology, because of its intimate relationship with medicine brings up specific disciplinary concerns over what collaboration might actually entail. Studies about particular diseases, like cancer, have previously raised concerns because they often entail a narrowing of focus and collaboration across disciplines and with biomedicine in particular. This process is evident in what Browner (1999) has called the "medicalization of medical anthropology." The concern is that researchers may become overly specialized in the same ways that medical practitioners specialize, so that our own thinking may become reductive and decontextualized. In some ways this concern is similar to the late black feminist, lesbian radical scholar Audre Lorde's (1984) argument that "the master's tools will never dismantle the master's house." We cannot use the same hegemonic mode of thinking to create change, to contribute new approaches and theories or unravel taken for granted processes and knowledges.

The fact that many medical anthropologists often have positions in schools of medicine, nursing, or public health or sometimes work for health-research centers or government agencies, reveals an on-going struggle to engage and value issues of difference and develop a social medicine, rather than science and medicine constituting a decontextualized definition of social difference. I, for one, wholeheartedly agree with Browner's concerns. In the specificity of my decades long dance with cancer research I have had more fruitful and fulfilling opportunities for collaboration across disciplines; with physicians, psychologists, sociologists, epidemiologists, nutritionists, and public health researchers, with community organizations and their leaders, with other anthropologists and with students who did not know that you could put an anthropological lens to cancer. However, these opportunities for collaboration and the dominance of biomedical understandings of the body do cause concern and lead me to disengage from such work. Crossing disciplinary boundaries, or entering the "master's house" is always fraught with concerns over the potential hegemonic influences that biomedicine might have on my anthropological practice and knowledge, I worry that I have become a "handmaiden" in the service of a singular view of human life. And then I wonder whose voice is speaking here? Is my concern only about being silenced by the voice of hegemony or is there another dominant voice that is pushing a particular way of doing one's work, a practice that limits the extent to which inclusivity should be engaged? Ultimately, there is a tension between the concerns of the biomedical field homogenizing or disciplining our discipline — and our own discipline's disciplining of scholars who engage in collaborative work.

Disciplines and Disciplining Difference

There are many epistemological and methodological differences between biomedical and anthropological thinking. I do not want to reiterate those issues here, but rather, following Strathern's work on "audit cultures" (2000) and interdisciplinarity (2004), I want to think about the institutional accounting — those strategies used to govern the scholarship within disciplinary boundaries (such as funding and publishing and how these are enforced by our peers). These accounting techniques serve to extend mechanisms that further entrench disciplinary boundaries that make collaborative interdisciplinary work a threat to scholars' livelihood. For example, while I worked in the medical school I learned that a single author book is valued less than multiple authored articles. Multiple author articles are valued more because they show that the lead author is able to bring together a strong research team, that multiple facets of questions are discussed, researched, and considered by all of the collaborators. In an ideal working environment, there is opportunity for a diversity of thought and innovation. It is assumed that the lead researcher is actively mentoring individuals who are in the early stages of their careers. Providing mentees with opportunities to engage in research and publication processes fosters their future success. In contrast, single author articles demonstrate that the individual is clearly the generator of an idea, data collection, and is capable of following multiple strands of an argument. In the case of single authors, more value is also given because it is assumed that the experience of being in the field with the researcher's interlocutors gives more insight and knowledge about the social processes he or she is describing. In addition, the researcher because they have not been distracted by a multiplicity of people and ideas, is able to think more deeply about their chosen topic. These two assumptions about what disciplines and authorship mean are, as my mentor would have it, part of the tension between following an anthropological pursuit of the "exotic" or the collaborative interdisciplinary trajectory that a research career in cancer would provide. The questions that interdisciplinarity raise have to do with its ambiguity, the way it troubles the categories of disciplinary selves and others that are maintained, in part, through accounting techniques. I would also like to argue that the distinct differences with which disciplines value collaboration have implications for minority women because of the intersectionality of race, class and gender and its application in academia. Claims of set criteria are made all too frequently as the careers of academics are regularly judged, evaluated, reviewed, and held in the hands of their peers and of those who know their discipline in very specific ways. These evaluations are made ever more complicated as academics, typically younger minority scholars, are choosing to pursue research that is interdisciplinary and intimately engaged with local community needs. When there are no clear bodies of disciplinary knowledge, premier journals with a long history of publication, nor a myriad of forms for inclusivity in authorship, how does the academy count excellence?

I raise these questions as they reflect my own struggles with collaborative and interdisciplinary activities and the persistence with which I hear colleagues and the students that I mentor who suffer from disciplinary inflexibility regarding our intentions to create a career that reflects our intellectual and personal values. The reader, to this point, may think that among the two choices that the mentor laid out for me, I chose to continue working in the arena of cancer inequalities, with large interdisciplinary collaborative research groups. If that is the assumption, you would be right. You would also be right if you assumed that I had chosen to conduct my own research with Native Hawaiians on the links between health and sovereignty. In the beginning one project was a symbol of my passion and the other provided me with research skills and paid the bills. Both projects were always in honor of my heritage. As time went on both projects have become my passion and it is unclear to me how to do one and not the other. Both projects scream of social injustice and beckon me to engage. This trajectory has also caused a host of contradictory opinions when my academic file is evaluated as I have both continued with the same area of research throughout my career and have not continued in the same area of research. I have enough and don't have enough scholarship in the "proper" venues, of single authored articles, of grant money, and any other measure with which I am evaluated. Some people tolerate or approve of my direction and others absolutely disapprove. So what might we make of scholars who have intentionally chosen dual efforts with contradictory expectations?

Measures of Excellence

There are two areas that are unquestionable measures of excellence, extramural funding and publishing. Regardless of the discipline, scholars, particularly in difficult economic times, are encouraged to apply for funding. As stated previously, the meaning of funding varies across discipline and although the university views large multi-million dollar grants as a clear sign of "excellence" that same grant has implications within individual disciplines. For my discipline, there are still concerns about using the master's tools. For example, Simon Lee (2009) analyzed social scientists NIH grant submissions that responded to calls for research proposals focusing on health inequalities. Lee found that instead of questioning categories of race and ethnicity as the basis for research design those same categories are reified. The result is that the focus of the research is too narrowly defined and creates cultural dimensions as "problematic" (DiGiacomo, 1999) rather than targeting larger issues such as access. Ultimately, by contributing to the documentation of "beliefs" and practices, our work may end up contributing to the ever-increasing surveillance and control of people and populations by government and institutions (Foucault, 1977). As an anthropologist I find these critiques troubling, to the extent that we have any control over our work once it has been published, the last thing I would want to participate in anyone's subjugation.

And yet, participating and being awarded with large interdisciplinary grants afford enormous opportunities across the spectrum of a career. Two of the key opportunities that grant funding provided entailed community building and fostering the careers of graduate and undergraduate students. Having worked in a research institute I failed to remember that academic departments were quite solitary. I had grown accustomed to having a group of people who were interested in similar issues working through a shared agenda. While there may be a department out there that works in similar ways, this was not the case for me in my first academic department. Thus returning to the work of extramural funding, for me, was the perfect mechanism to build the kind of intellectual engagement that I cherish. I was able to find colleagues in different disciplines and well as colleagues in my own discipline who were not in anthropology departments. Through these projects we could engage our differences, discover aspects of our work that had been silenced, and maintain a critical eye so that our attention to the structural forces was always addressed. Importantly we created a community to support each other in our research and personal lives.

From the outside, however, this work takes on a different form. The method and assumptions of the work are different and scholars who intentionally do not want to work in that frame read the critiques of "biomedicine's handmaidens" which leads to a categorization of not quite "doing anthropology." The second issue with obtaining large grants is that in my case it slowed down efforts to write single author papers because I was either managing the grant or I was working on writing papers with colleagues or graduate students. Again, the focus was on the team rather than the individual. The problem for women and minority scholars is that this process is recast into a supportive role and hence not valued. I spent so much time trying to assist others that my own work suffered (that is, my own individual writing and research, but not that of the collaborative). Indeed, I had a colleague who was so bewildered by how those of us who had NIH grants had to organize our work she thought that an ethnographic study needed to be done on us. The collaborative researcher is now made "exotic." Despite the value of extramural funding at the university level, that value does not necessarily carry across the various hierarchies and recognized as fitting disciplinary criteria.

In the early 1990s Scheper-Hughes (1990) suggested that untenured professors not engage in collaborative efforts. This suggestion was made in part because of threats to gaining a strong foundation in anthropological thinking, but also, I suspect, because of the questions that it raises about the accountability in publishing. Publications represent the final step in the production of knowledge and disciplinary engagement. We are concerned not only with the quality and number of articles, but also the venues. What does it mean to have an anthropologist publishing in medical journals, psychological journals or any other non-anthropological journals? Are these the venues that build a national or international reputation for anthropologists? Are these the venues that lead to recognition for a department? That bring in graduate students? That advance knowledge in the field? Furthermore, as Strathern (2005) has asked, what does it mean to have one perspective with multiple authors? How can we know how to categorize these articles within a discipline? If you have a single author then it is clear that it is the product of an individual mind — which makes me wonder exactly when the production of knowledge ever really attributable to one mind. So, how do we account for the conversations, the editing, the work of our disciplinary colleagues, or how do we account for the knowledge work of community members (including them as co-authors is an increasing practice that I have engaged in on numerous occasions). Thus authorship is as much about the productivity of individuals as it is about the creation of disciplinary boundaries and receiving "credit" for your contribution.

Whether or not an individual scholar engages in this type of writing depends on their intentions for their career. I intend for biomedicine to consider the multiple facets of the lives of the patients they see. Our lives are too valuable to be decontextualized in the way that a pure biomedical perspective would pursue. There is a larger issue at stake, that is the participation of social scientists in general and anthropologists in particular in multi-authored papers can change the meaning of the specifics of a biomedical agenda. For instance, we can turn a conversation on "fatalism" about prospects for cancer survival in minority communities from a simplified discussion of knowledge deficit and cultural barriers to a nuanced and contextualized discussion of the political economy of health. A critical perspective provides the reasons why when communities have little medical access, low incomes, and face discrimination — they contextualize cancer as an automatic death sentence. Could I achieve these perspectives in single authored publications? Absolutely. The cost, however, involves erasing the voices of people who contributed to the intellectual process. It means that when I could have provided an opportunity for that person to write a section of an article, to include another voice, I actively chose to silence them. Sometimes the choice is difficult. There are times where I do the majority of the work, and yet when my colleagues read the publication record and see multiple names, they are far too casual about dismissing my contributions. On the flip side, there are articles where someone expected to be included, but they did not do any of the writing or contribute. In these cases I feel no compulsion to include them. If my goal is to reduce inequity, to make room for other voices to be heard, then having a publishing record that mirrors one in the biological sciences but means something completely different is part of the cost. These are the reasons why I continue to engage in collaborative interdisciplinary work. It is with the hope of making an impact within the conversation that I am having with academics interested in the topic I am researching and creating opportunities for a plethora of voices. Is that not a measure of moving the discipline forward?

I often get discouraged because within my own discipline I often feel like an outsider. It is possible that many of us feel this way regardless of the specifics of our topic or discipline. It is encouraging to find like-minded scholars who want to collaborate on grants, books, and articles. While my dual career may seem strange to colleagues, I have found that there are many of us out there. Some people engage in multiple projects not because they cannot decide what their own focus is supposed to be, but rather they are engaged in blurring the boundaries of what work and thoughts are supposed to look like, because we believe both in our freedom to create a career of our choosing and, more importantly, where it is in the gaps between the disciplines that interesting questions occur.

Intentionally Liminal

Would it be a good ending if I was to simply say, be liminal in your career? As if somehow that will sustain us in our careers as we amble through. No, we must be intentionally liminal. It is imperative that a scholar always have a clear vision of her work, the understanding that she is the director of that work, and that she lay claim to the choices she has made for her career, because ultimately someone will attempt to lay claim and redefine what she has done. Early on in my postdoctoral years I attended a conference that was to provide career advice to recent Ph.D.s. Topics included how to manage the balance between one's personal and academic life, publishing, grant writing, creating your curriculum vitae and the like. One of the keynote speakers addressed the issue of discrimination in academia. Her talk was passionate. The battle fatigue of being a minority woman and the everyday discriminations that we encounter were evident. In spite of everything that she had said, all I could remember her saying was that when you are attacked, you need to "just cut them off at the knees." Take the attacker down, call that person out on their biases and do not allow yourself to be denigrated.

When I came back from the conference I was surprised at how unsettled I was by her talk. It's not that I don't know that discrimination occurs in academia or that I don't think that such disrespectful behavior should not be confronted. But how was I to take that information "just cut them off at the knees"? I am not a loud or confrontational person. It is necessary to talk about discrimination and to have strategies to deal with its occurrence. Indeed actively discussing discrimination is key to changing inequity. But how would "cutting people off at the knees" play out for me? Would I even be the subject of discriminatory words aimed at diminishing me and my work? What would such a situation look like? Was there not something else that I could do that is more in line with my personality, without sacrificing my principles and self-respect? After relaying this story, my mentor at the time told me that yes, those things happen and would probably happen to me. But rather than worry about it, that I should just do my work. That way people can say whatever they want but your work will stand and that is what will move you through the academic ranks. I will always feel a bit ambivalent about this advice because it seems to overlook active measures to take in the face of discrimination, and that sometimes just doing your work is not enough. Nonetheless, this message felt like something that I could actually manage. At the end of the day, we fight against our detractors if we have to with words, but mainly we combat them with our knowledge.

As I look back on my career there have always been silly and insensitive things that people say that are meant to undermine my knowledge and the intentionality with which I direct my career. These statements ranged from gossip or musings about my sexual life, that male mentors were paternal towards me, or that I was "too young" for the level of research, service or mentoring in which I was engaged. In talking with many of my fellow female and minority colleagues, these statements are all too common in the course of their careers. On the surface we might brush this off, as I often did, as the silly things people say. Interestingly, these statements are able to gain more weight when a scholar engages in collaborative and interdisciplinary work. Notions of being "too young" or somehow not being the sole genitor of your work have provided fodder for the few people who would like to see my career stagnate or even fail. These statements are made in order to infantilize the scholar and the collaborative efforts in which he or she engages. Because I had chosen to work collaboratively, because I had chosen to publish in anthropology and non-anthropology journals, because I spent time supporting students and colleagues outside of my discipline I suddenly became "too young." We need only look back to the caricatures of colonized peoples to see that infantilizing the efforts and protests of brown people is an all too common practice. But I had done my work, and while hurt by the words of a few, the majority of my department and the campus saw my accomplishments. They recognized and acknowledged that while it was not the typical route of a cultural anthropologist, that my intentions had been recognized inside and outside of my discipline.

I tell this story not to discourage interdisciplinary and collaborative work, but rather to recognize how the different expectations between disciplinary work can become infused with meanings that can also undermine our efforts. We must also acknowledge that even though only a couple of people engage in infantilizing behavior, this is an act of bullying and ultimately had the power of bullying in my own experience. When these statements were made, they had the effect of making me feel like everyone believed what was being said about me. The purpose of bullying is to alienate an individual and in silencing that person that they will ultimately leave. For me, however, having a dual research program saved me from this alienation and continues to drive my efforts. It has provided me with a host of colleagues who share intellectual questions, research agendas, and personal trials. It has also allowed me to engage with numerous students and foster their careers as scholars who continue to question and advance our knowledge and activism around inequity.

The joyous and difficult encounters in academia may have not played out the way they did if I had not been encouraged to clearly understand the critiques and my motivations for engaging in multiple projects. Upon entering the job market my postdoctoral mentor, Carole Browner, was reviewing my letters of application. Since I had recently finished my Ph.D. it was clear to her that I had two ongoing projects. She told me "Juliet, if you're going to have multiple projects, you need to tell people a story that connects it altogether." I have used this advice in all of my letters and I think it works regardless of whether you're a recent Ph.D. or someone who has been in academia for decades. Because my two projects were based in two seemingly different ways of working and asked different questions about health (one collaborative and one solitary) it was important to show that these were not disjointed questions. I needed to show that my dual projects were not the outcome of someone who could not make up their mind and was tossed to and fro by the desires of others, but rather that they revealed a clear trajectory in intellectual thought. What she was telling me was that I needed to show intentionality in my career. My critique is not that accountability in academia exists. I cannot yet imagine a social world in which these things don't come to matter in some shape or form. My critique or questions are as follows: What do we do when confronted with gender and racial assumptions that are so thoroughly woven into the hierarchy? And what do we do with our colleagues who embrace inclusivity at levels that disrupt disciplinary accountings as a matter of knowledge production and change? In the end, this is a moral question about how we deal with difference.

NOTES

1. Here I reference Richard Rodriguez's work *Brown: The Last Discovery of America.* "Brown bleeds through the straight line, unstaunchable — the line separating black from white, for example. Brown confuses. Brown forms at the border of contradiction (the ability of language to express two or several things at once, the ability of bodies to experience two or several things at once)" (2002:xi).

2. See McMullin 2010:55–56 for a more detailed explanation of my father's categorization as Hawaiian.

REFERENCES

Browner, C. (1999). On the medicalization of medical anthropology. *Medical Anthropology Quarterly. 13*(2), 135–140.

DiGiacomo, S. (1999). Can there be a "cultural epidemiology"? *Medical Anthropology Quarterly.* 13(4), 436–457.

Lee, CJS. (2009). Science, surveillance, and the politics of redress in health disparities research. *Race/Ethnicity: Multidisciplinary Global Perspectives 3,* 51–74.

Lorde, A. (1984). The master's tools will never dismantle the master's house. In A. Lorde (Ed.), *Sister outsider: Essays and speeches.* (pp. 110–113). Berkeley, CA: Crossing.

McMullin, J. (2010). *The healthy ancestor: Embodied inequality and the revitalization of native hawaiian health.* Walnut Creek, CA: Left Coast.

Rodriguez, R. (2002). *Brown: The last discovery of America.* New York: Penguin.

Scheper-Hughes, N. (1990). Three propositions for a critically applied medical anthropology. *Social Science and Medicine. 30*(2), 189–197.

Strathern, M. (2000). *Audit cultures: Anthropological studies in accountability, ethics and the academy*. London: Routledge.

Strathern, M. (2004). *Commons + borderlands: Working papers on interdisciplinarity, accountability and the flow of knowledge*. Oxon: Sean Kingston.

Strathern, M. (2005). *Partial connections*. Walnut Creek, CA: Altamira.

An Open Letter on
How to Succeed in
Academic Life

JUDITH LIU

I attended graduate school at a Research-1 institution and received a first-rate education that provided excellent scholarly and research training from top-notched sociology scholars. Although I refer to some of my professors as mentors, in reality, what I received was help in negotiating graduate school processes, but this help provided little in the way of understanding what being a faculty member actually entailed. Absent was the one-on-one interaction from a "wise and trusted counselor."

When I arrived as a new faculty member at the University of San Diego, I knew little about existing departmental and campus dynamics and almost nothing about promotion and tenure procedures. Wanting to do more than just survive but to thrive at my institution, I realized that integrating into the campus and creating social networks was crucial — success meant becoming part of a community. Coming from a discipline that has community building as one of its principal tenets, my attraction to sociology was due in part to my own quest to "belong." Born and raised in a Brooklyn tenement in a predominantly Puerto Rican and African American area and later, moving to an Italian and Jewish neighborhood in the Bronx, we were the only "Orientals" in our community. But living amongst racial, ethnic, and religious diversity also provided rich and meaningful relationships and a healthy dose of survival skills that have served me well in recognizing the importance of community and what it takes to carve out a life in an environment where it is not evident how I "belong."

"Are all academics depressed?" a good friend and fellow academic once asked me in earnest. After looking around at his own institution and thinking about his colleagues nationwide, he struggled to come up with even a handful of academics who were not "depressed, disillusioned or in despair." Since he considered me none of the above, he wanted my advice. It was a cause for pause. After some reflection, my thoughts about academia are that we are drawn to the academy and the disciplines we choose. Control over one's own time and research, the energy created by an intellectual environment, the desire to have an impact, renown, travel or the comfort of a cloistered environment are some reasons we are drawn to the profession. However, because there is no "job training" once we arrive, the learning curve is steep and that is when the cloistered environment begins to feel more like a total institution than the haven we envisioned. Unless academia is truly a profession of the disaffected, what can be done to lessen depression, disillusionment, and despair?

In my own path, I have sought and worked with individuals who have helped me at various stages of my life and in my career. Thus, the most valuable message I can send to those who are beginning their careers is to create a community by finding mentors and allies, individuals who truly will serve two vital functions: professional development and social-psychological support.

Winding one's way through the academic maze and creating a community are made easier with mentors. These individuals can help turn the seemingly contested terrain into an environment based upon mutual support and respect.

Suggested Strategies for Success

A. On time.

Short of magically creating the eight-day week, finding the balance among work, writing, and relationships is always a challenge because the number one stressor in the modern world is not enough *time*. There never seems to be enough time to teach, advise/mentor students, conduct research, write, and still also have a life outside of the academy. Time spent with family and friends is frequently given short shrift; yet, time is the most valuable asset we possess.

My reality check came when I was chair of the department and spending long hours seven days a week while constantly losing track of time. Staying at times beyond midnight, my spouse first insisted on chauffeuring me to school on weekends. Then he refused to wait until I completed a "five minute administrative errand" because they turned out to be five minutes of the hour hand. But when a colleague accused me of holding secret weekend departmental meetings (patently false since I was scarcely successful in getting faculty to attend meetings *during* the week), I knew I was spending too much time in the office. As the chair, my research and publication plans were not just "put on the back burner," the pot was not even in the kitchen. Scheduling a routine, setting priorities, and handling one crisis at a time were the only things that saved me.

B. Design a multi-year plan.

Begin with a realistic personal multi-year timeline based upon your institution's retention, promotion, and tenure process. What does the institution require for retention, tenure, and promotion? Consider what it will take to meet those demands. Although requirements for publications vary significantly from type of institution (i.e., research versus teaching) and discipline, research and publication requirements exist at some level in all institutions. As a freshly minted Ph.D. arriving at my institution, the teaching load was 4/4 where faculty members were considered to be teachers first; consequently, the publication requirements were less stringent than they are currently with a 3/3 load where new faculty members are considered to be teacher-scholars. Other criteria such as "Service to the University and Community" played a stronger role in the review process, and serving on committees both on and off campus was weighted more.

Include in this multi-year timeline important items such as conference dates, "deadlines" to complete writing projects, journal deadline dates. Update the multi-year timeline regularly.

multi-year plan

C. Avoid the "loss mentality."

Having a timeline helps in avoiding the "loss mentality." Learn how to "just say no" to those enticing opportunities that suddenly appear. Rarely are these opportunities truly the "chance of a lifetime." If one does appear, take it; otherwise assess realistically. Questions to ask are: How will this opportunity affect my multi-year plan? Can this opportunity lead to a conference paper and/or a publication? What priorities must be shifted in the multi-year plan to accommodate this opportunity? What impact will this opportunity have on my physical and mental well-being? Conducting an honest cost/benefit analysis will help in the decision-making process. Here is where mentors and allies can provide more dispassionate perspectives. Taking the attitude that every opportunity not taken is a short-term "loss" will lead to long-term over-commitment. Always ask yourself: "What is the main goal?" And keep in mind that your answer must be: "Tenure."

D. Professional Conferences and Papers

Make everything do double-duty. Attend regional and specialized conferences that have their own journals (for example, in Sociology, the Pacific Sociological Association and the Coalition of Urban and Metropolitan Universities each have their own journals). Submit a proposal, write a paper, obtain feedback from the session, and send the revised paper to that journal.

Consider how a similar paper can be submitted to another conference. There has been a mindset shift. In the past, submitting a previously presented paper to another conference might have been considered inappropriate. During recent searches at USD, however, candidates have indicated that their papers have been presented at multiple conferences and can be regarded as an indication of the innovation and interest in the topic. For example, writing about pedagogical innovation can be presented and published both within your discipline and another conference focused on pedagogy (e.g., American Association of Colleges and University [AACU] has multiple panels on pedagogy).

E. Avoid "rescue creep."

Fresh from my graduate school experiences, I was especially vulnerable to "rescue creep" and took on increasingly more commitments.

Students lined-up at the door; unthinkable stories were confided to me in the confines of my office; students and colleagues wept in my office; the telephone rang off the hook. Each of these problems required time to "get my head around the situation" in order to figure out how to solve them. I realized that rescuing everyone was untenable. I needed to learn to "triage" — the act of distinguishing between a real emergency that requires immediate attention and a situation that may need attention, but not at this moment. Learning to defer non-emergency situations is an important skill.

Mentors and allies can help you distinguish the difference between trying to rescue and actually assisting a student by providing the all important larger perspective that we may lose sight of when we are caught up in the immediacy of the moment.

F. Avoid the "technology trap."

Technology is the Janus-faced boon and bane of our existence. The technological devices that are now iconic of our culture are not necessarily "labor-saving devices." While they have simplified the drudgery, they have, in many ways, increased our work. In order to minimize their disruptive nature, designate a set time each day to go through e-mails to catch up on the "sweet poison" of social media, and to answer missed telephone calls.

Disrupt the "on-call" mentality by charting the number calls, texts, and e-mails received in a day; the number will be sobering and can provide "data" for how much time is spent on responding to the various media. Each one is an interruption that can sabotage any momentum you may have on maintaining your multi-year plan. Avoid telephone tag by being specific in text and voice messages as to your time availability and request the same from any caller.

Be cautious about social media networks. Even though I do not have a Facebook account, aspects of my life are all over the net because other people have posted pictures and written about me. What might appear to be an innocent post can be taken out of context and come back to haunt. Olympic Gold Medal winner Michael Phelps did not post the party pictures where he was seen smoking a bong. He was outed by a "friend." Reappointment and tenure have been denied based upon information obtained from Facebook. The faculty member who has the reputation for "always being on Facebook" at the expense of all else will not acquire necessary academic creditability.

G. What to be on time for:

• Be punctual to class.

Constantly running late for class may have the unintended consequence of having students draw the conclusion that you are either disorganized or lackadaisical about your commitment to teaching. When one faculty member was denied reappointment, chronic tardiness to class noted in student evaluations was one of the justifications. In defense, the faculty member used an "ethnic time" explanation claiming that it was part of her culture to be late. Really? That was a self-inflicted wound that proved terminal to her chances for reappointment.

If anything, consider arriving to class early. Some of the best conversations and discussions occur *before* class begins when students are more relaxed and talkative.

• Meetings with those in the chain of command.

It goes without saying, but I am saying it nonetheless, do not be late for meetings with the chair, the dean or the provost. Better to hurry up and wait than to have the awkwardness of apologizing for being tardy. Make no mistake: each encounter provides data for those who will be evaluating you. Develop the reputation for being on time because having a "good reputation" provides social margin and can serve as a buffer for those times when you will be late. It is far better to surprise people by being early than to surprise them by being tardy.

H. What to make time for:

• Personal Time.

When a colleague recently died suddenly of a massive coronary midway during a year-long sabbatical, it caused many faculty members to reflect upon their own lives—start exercising, stop smoking, diet, implement stress reduction. My epiphany came much earlier when my brother had his first stroke in his mid-fifties. I sought something sustainable to improve my health. What I found was *tai qi*. When I was a child, I was fascinated while watching my father go through the form.

108

As the son of a warlord, requisite military training necessitated that my father learn *tai qi* beginning at age four. I witnessed him flatten and disarm a knife-wielding mugger at age seven, and my desire to learn *tai qi* was forged in that moment, but because I was a "girl," my very traditional father would not teach me. When the local YMCA offered *tai qi* lessons, I took the leap. Twice weekly, I now schedule time to take lessons from a fifth generation *tai qi* master who has taught me so much more than just the form. Flowing the form with others in yet another community has taught me persistence, perseverance, and patience.

Create personal time for friends and family. Schedule a weekly "date" night for friends, spouse, and family; create a daily ritual for spending time with children. Resist the temptation to "skip it" because of time constraints.

• Committees

Junior faculty members are often tapped to serve on committees and feel vulnerable because they do not know what impact their refusal will have. Since there continues to be considerable confusion as to what will be counted/discounted in the tenure review process, understandably, anxiety and confusion abound.

Haunted by the admonition that refusing to take on yet another time-consuming committee assignment might mean that the voice of those who shared my perspective might go unheard, I felt "obligated" to accept the call to serve whenever I was asked. When committees on diversity, inclusion, race, ethnicity, and gender were created, I was one of the "usual suspects." The only time I was able to relinquish these obligations was when I was went on sabbatical.

How many of us, however, have been "put on the spot" to serve on a committee? We are all made "offers we cannot refuse"— those that come from the dean, provost or president — and serving on these committees is important because they provide social connections, contacts with faculty and professional staff across campus, and produce high visibility. We also get requests to serve on committees or do work in the community through unofficial channels. Resist the temptation to accept no matter how important the request may seem or how flattered you feel by being asked. Have the department chair serve as a "buffer." At these moments, the response must be, "I must clear any requests with my chair." Discussing the request with the chair also serves the purpose of bringing to light just how many requests come to faculty members in the department.

• Be visible

At USD, the president hosts an annual convocation and holiday party; the provost has instituted campus-wide receptions throughout the year; the college dean organizes the college holiday and end-of-the-year party. These are important events to attend. It is not only an opportunity to celebrate with others across campus, it is also an opportunity to reconnect with old friends and meet new colleagues. These occasions also provide the opportunity to be seen by key administrators at all levels of the institution. While not attending these events will not directly influence your retention and tenure at the institution, attendance at these functions provide "data" about your commitment to the institution and whether or not you are a "team player." The small investment in effort to attend these events is time well spent.

Do not underestimate the value of attending other functions such as sporting events, homecoming or graduation. These are high visibility occasions to meet and socialize with influential members of the campus community who are also in attendance but in a much more casual setting.

Develop an Institutional GPS System

Learn how to navigate the university's social and political landscape. Learn who to go through, who to go around, and who to go above. Go through the normal chain of command, but if one level says no, *escalate* to the next level. Be tenacious/persistent but always be pleasant. Taking out frustrations on the person who initially denies the request will neither solve the matter nor achieve the desired goal.

Consider the medium to be used. Starting with an e-mail is fine, but with each escalation, move from e-mail to telephone to in-person. It is easy to ignore e-mails and voice mail; it is much more difficult to say "no" in person. Never put anything in writing that is inflammatory or highly charged. I was once advised by a dean to wait "three days" before responding to a hostile e-mail. Answering in haste or in a confrontational, angry fashion will only fuel the issue. Waiting has the advantage of helping one to think about the situation and to make an informed decision by considering all sides. Rather than communicating through e-mail, a dispassionate face-to-face meeting or a telephone message will get better results.

Case in point. When I wanted to provide "scholarships" for seventh- to twelfth-grade teachers taking a USD sociology course, rather than going through the usual channels of financial aid or admissions, I spoke with professional staff at the continuing education office who at each successive level said "No." I kept notes on the encounters as a record of steps taken (a good strategy). I knew the director of the academic division, called him, and arranged a meeting. At this meeting, I pitched the proposal citing its academic and scholarly merits, USD's mission statement, how the proposal was consistent with current initiatives, and how such a small scholarship would enhance the university's reputation in the community. I was also poised to offer possible alternatives (ranging from reduced fees to providing a small number of scholarships) to each possible "No" response. Although the proposal was accepted, I was also fully prepared to escalate to the Provost and President levels if necessary.

Write On

When reviewing the multi-year plan, think publication pipeline: Given that the average turnaround time for an article is one-year, articles must be in the pipeline each year to meet publication requirements. "In process;" "under submission;" "revise and resubmit status" will NOT do; a tentative date of publication is what tenure committees are seeking. Begin with a target date and work backwards to design the timeline accordingly.

A. Create a sacrosanct "writing space."

Writing is a "messy" process, at least for me — it involves piles of papers everywhere; books smashed face down; notes scratched on bits of paper that are scattered about. Without a non-designated writing space, so much time is wasted just trying to find what we need.

If the designated space is at home, nothing other than writing can be done in there. Distinguish between "public" (dining, living, family space) and "private" (desk, office) space; do not encroach into public space.

If it is on campus, close your door and post a "Do not disturb sign." There is a knock on the door. Do you answer it? NO. Develop a "secret knock" if it is truly an emergency. (Mine is "Shave and a haircut; two bits.") The telephone rings. Do you answer it? NO. Return the calls during a designated time. If you have the luxury of a telephone that can be switched to voice-mail, do so. A colleague spies you in the hallway. Do you stop and chat? Of course, but keep it brief. A student stops you in the hallway. Do you stop and chat? A brief greeting will do, but for anything else, inform the student that you are unavailable at this time.

Personally, I find working on campus too distracting. There are a hundred and one things that can entice me away from the task at hand. Home (although it, too, has so many tasks that can divert attention) is a better environment for me because I can choose to ignore things more easily and focus on what needs to be done.

B. Set a goal.

Set a specific goal for each writing session, and abide by it.

Take breaks, but confine the number and duration of them or the time will slip away. Avoid momentum busters caused by multi-tasking — answering that "quick" telephone call or shooting out "a couple" of e-mails divert your attention.

If you are working on campus, and a student asks you a "quick advising question," do you answer it? NO. Advising can suck up tremendous amounts of time especially during what invariably is the busiest time of the school term. Schedule specific student advising times; highlight those times in a special section of your syllabi; post them prominently on your office door; and announce them in all classes especially during registration periods. Only genuine emergencies should be handled off schedule. Better yet, establish this procedure as a departmental policy. For all others, as harsh as it may feel, the response must be to have the student return during the scheduled advising time.

C. Color code projects.

Organize each writing project separately by color and box. Label everything. Re-file each day to avoid losing materials—I spend so much time just looking for things, and doing so inevitably makes me both furious and anxious. If you have the luxury of a private space, cover it so that any air current or errant pet does not scatter or eat the materials. I once had a cat that could not resist taking a running leap into the most important pile of papers spread laying on the floor and then proceed to smack down the fluttering papers and chew them up.

D. Set a schedule.

Writing first thing in the morning worked best for me. Thus, from 6:45 to noon was the designated time for writing with a set goal of writing a minimum of TWO pages per day. I took breaks, but kept to the schedule. From noon to 3:00, I set aside time to complete other tasks. One afternoon a week was designated for running errands; another for laundry; another for cleaning. Clustering together responsibilities helped me maintain a regular schedule so that I could finish a book project in nine months.

E. Join or create a writing group.

I belong to three writing groups, two of which serve a social psychological function. We do not read each other's work; what we do is provide professional advice — when to hire an agent or publicist; upcoming events; writing opportunities. The other is one that has been created on campus. The "Scholarship of Teaching and Learning" [SoTL] group meets once a month with one or two designated pieces submitted by members. Others in the group read, critique, and provide suggestions/recommendations/corrections. Writing groups serve an important function of pushing to meet "deadlines."

On Burn Out

Professional interests, research opportunities, enthusiasm for teaching, and our attitudes toward our institutions will go through a cycle of ebbs and flows. Once the "battle" for tenure has been successfully waged, reframe the discourse from one of "warfare" and survival to one of career building and thriving. Maintaining the "siege" metaphor merely perpetuates the battle mentality; small wonder that we suffer "battle fatigue." Although I am NOT a proponent of "positive thinking," language is powerful, and by changing the discourse from one of surviving to one of thriving, it can have a profound impact on how to plan for the future.

A. Find a passion and pursue it.

What energized my career was working in the Center for Community Service-Learning. My foray into community service-learning came through a pedagogical path when I was seeking ways to improve my teaching. I stayed because I found an intellectual and personal space where I could thrive. Committed, dedicated students and professional staff work at the center. They are allies who helped me weather any number of swells that could have swamped me along my career path. Thus, whenever I enter the center, I am revived by the enthusiasm and energy of the occupants. As a consequence, I have also published a number of articles related to community service-learning.

B. Be a mentor and ally.

Finding mentors and allies is essential for surviving and thriving at an institution. Being a mentor or ally is equally important. For either role, choose carefully. These individuals must be discreet—people who will not repeat any information given in confidence. The campus is a cloistered environment where secrets are difficult to keep. Develop the reputation for not engaging in information mongering or inadvertently passing along sensitive information. Do not share information with anyone on campus that you do not wish others to know. Cultivate people who can keep confidences.

One caveat: Chairs cannot be expected to serve as mentors because they cannot be both the steward of the department *and* a personal champion without creating a potential conflict of interest. Also, if any personality/professional clashes occur, junior faculty members are placed in an even more untenable situation vis-à-vis more senior faculty members.

Trust and discretion are essential. In two of the writing groups to which I belong, we have an ESAD policy—"Eat Shit and Die"—if any one of us divulges information about what has been shared in confidence within the group. I evoke the same rule with those whom I work. Violate it and our non-professional relationship ends. Period.

The short benefit of being an ally with and/or mentoring junior faculty members is working with energetic, enthusiastic, and exciting colleagues who can serve as a catalyst for new ideas and projects. The long term benefit is not only the satisfaction of helping one generation navigate the turbulent tenure seas, but also the possibility of establishing a relationship that endures the test of time. To this day, there are colleagues, long retired who I continue to see on a regular basis. They are part of my "community of memory" and help provide perspective and advice.

In the end, obtaining tenure is not merely about surviving the process, but learning how to thrive in the environment of our choosing. Only by successfully navigating the tenure process do we have the possibility of "paying it forward" by becoming mentors and allies for the next generation and helping others by making the academic world less of an arena and more of a community. The bottom line is, no matter how gifted a teacher, mentor, researcher you are, if you are *not* around, everyone loses.

Creating the Perfect Storm

Making the Best Case for Promotion and Tenure

TONI GRIEGO JONES

Years ago when I came to the University of the Southwest, I had great expectations for research and publication, I was excited at the prospect of mentoring doctoral students and above all, was thrilled to be joining faculty who were world renowned for their research in my field. I even aspired to be a full professor but, very quickly, my self-confidence as a researcher, teacher, and competent professional was eroding. Being a woman of color, I had not gotten into the ranks of the professoriate without experiencing some racism and sexism, but this was different. The deep current of political intrigue, biases, and outright hostility toward women faculty, particularly women faculty of color, steadily dragged me under even as I naively believed that I was contributing to my department and university. Here I describe how I surfaced and kept afloat in the dirty waters of academia. Simply put, it is a story of organizing women faculty of color into a powerful, tough and successful network at a large, public Research I university. This essay offers some suggestions for organizing, but its main purpose is to describe the work of a wise, empathetic, practical network of minority women faculty who learned something about making the perfect storm in academia, that is, about successfully putting together the elements that produce the best case for promotion and tenure.

Several years into my tenure at the university I was asked to be the

116

chair of a very contentious department in my college. At the time the department was locked in mortal combat with the dean. They had been at odds long before I arrived and there was deep conflict among department faculty as well. Believing that I could facilitate communication between the department faculty and their arch enemy, the dean, I agreed to do this. After a few months in this position a colleague (also new to the department) told me she saw that I was getting eaten up by the dean and department faculty and she thought I really needed to talk with someone from the Association for Women Faculty to get some perspective and advice. My own work was suffering and herein is a word of advice to junior faculty or newly tenured faculty. Achieve the faculty rank you desire before taking on administrative positions. These situations eat up your time and cannot help but make enemies of people who may be in positions to hurt you later on. This experience itself was a good lesson in what not to do as a new faculty member, especially if you are a member of a marginalized group.

I had never been much interested in joining women's organizations, but I did have lunch with the president of the Association for Women Faculty and to my surprise, I found a kindred soul who shared with me the value of organizing women for a particular purpose. Thus, in 2003 I invited as many minority women faculty as I could find across campus to discuss equity treatment issues specifically related to our status as minority women faculty. This initial meeting resulted in the formation of an energetic network we named the Minority Women Faculty (MWF). These faculty decided then and there that their main focus would be supporting each other in the promotion and tenure process. They also decided that, although they were in agreement with the broader goals of the Association for Women Faculty, they wanted to function as an independent network focused on the experiences and issues of underrepresented women faculty of color in a large research university.

Through the years the Minority Women Faculty network also began to serve a second purpose besides supporting minority faculty through the process of promotion and tenure. The MWF became the recognized "voice" for minority women faculty in university-wide conversations about equity and diversity. MWF now has a seat at the University President's Diversity Coalition and is recognized by campus administrators as a voice representing perspectives of minority women faculty. This is important because discussions at the University Diversity Coalition, although about equity and promoting diversity in general, often did not include the double "whammy" of being minority and a woman when discrimination was concerned. Even though white women and minority men were supportive of minority women, the double whammy aspect was not always recognized and addressed.

In addition to talking with the president at meetings of the Diversity Coalition, the MWF also scheduled their own annual meetings with the president where minority women faculty could talk with the president alone about their issues and concerns. Further, because promotion and tenure is the responsibility of the university provost, the group met regularly with the provost and the associate provost in charge of Academic Affairs. These meetings have been valuable in giving women faculty who feel marginalized in the university system access to the highest levels of administrators. The face-to-face meetings promoted awareness of issues that were not visible to those who have the authority to enable change. An example of an outcome from these meetings was a change in the university data collection which facilitated reporting the intersection of gender and race/ethnicity in all annual reports on personnel. Over the years MWF collaborated with the provost's office to provide luncheon sessions only for MWF members where the vice provost explained policies and procedures for promotion/tenure and where minority women faculty could ask questions not only about university procedures but about their own departmental contexts and situations. The vice provost also incorporated feedback and suggestions from minority women faculty into the university-wide sessions held annually for junior faculty.

Because the bottom line for MWF was their success as professors, the network focused their energies on supporting women through the promotion and tenure process. This process is often perceived as scary and hidden by marginalized groups. It is hidden in that those who are not in with the powers-that-be are left to figure out the process on their own. Many minority women felt alone and without mentorship from their department heads or senior faculty, most of whom were white males who, in fact, make up the majority of senior professors and

118

administrators in higher education. As is common in most universities, the promotion and tenure process was spelled out on the university website and there were annual workshops for junior professors on the process, but there was the feeling among women that there were unwritten rules about what counts or does not count and about how candidates should organize their materials in the most effective way to present their best case for promotion and tenure. When minority women expressed concern to their department heads or deans, administrators often stated that if faculty were doing their work, i.e., publishing, they would be fine. One problem for many minority women faculty, however, was that their own academic work often was in subject areas that did not appear to be valued by senior faculty or heads. For example, a number of minority women faculty were in ethnic studies or gender studies programs. Even when their academic focus was in "mainstream" areas, they did not believe they were getting the same attention and advice as their male counterparts when it came to how to put materials together. Many of the minority women faculty felt they were not getting the advice they needed, they wanted a support network and this was provided by MWF.

From the beginning, when the minority women faculty agreed that promotion and tenure was the most important focus for the network, they recognized that their group did not have a lot of expertise in the process. Only those who have gone through the process can really explain what is involved and how best to present their work; there were a precious few senior minority women faculty. Most MWF members felt they knew what they had to do in the actual work of research, teaching, and service to get promoted but lacked the inside knowledge of how to package their work when it came time to prepare and present their materials. The task of preparing and submitting materials for promotion and tenure is a most personal and vulnerable one, one that requires faculty to bare their souls and convince others that their work merits promotion and tenure. Minority women are not generally socialized to brag about themselves and their work interests are often marginalized so it is difficult for them to crow about their work. Furthermore, this part of the process tends to be secretive and many faculty who have achieved tenure do not share their materials with others.

Some of the minority women faculty who were coming up for their third and fifth year reviews (the time table at this university), were surprised that they should have been saving bits and pieces of their academic lives to put into their materials. At this university, the expectation was that faculty would submit file boxes with original publications, programs, letters of commendation, and all evidence of the scope and breadth of their work. Also, faculty had to provide evidence of how important their work was to others, aside from the external review letters which they, of course, could not see. What other commendations, awards, or recognition from peers in academia had they received? In some cases, women faculty had not even begun to compile their materials and were shocked that no one in their departments had told them they should be keeping and organizing materials even as they began their careers as assistant professors. At one of the first luncheon workshop sessions, one of the most valued activities of MWF, was sharing the "promotion and tenure boxes" of senior women faculty. All members of the network were extremely grateful for the opportunity to look through their promotion and tenure files to see how they were organized and what was in them. It helped those who hadn't been saving and organizing their papers as well as those who had been because everyone found new ideas about what they should include or about how to present materials. Junior faculty realized that others in their department or college didn't know all that they had done, and they weren't going to know if the faculty member didn't make it clear and show how important the work was. Senior women faculty stressed the importance of communicating with department chairs who are pivotal in the promotion and tenure process as they are the gatekeepers to information and they comprise the majority of those serving on promotion and tenure committees. Department chairs are still predominantly white men. This was a serious problem for some of the women faculty because they felt their department chairs were not taking responsibility for informing them of expectations and what they would be judged on at the end of their reviews and particularly at the end of their probation period.

Aside from encouraging and giving advice on how to communicate more aggressively with department chairs, MWF also realized that chairs themselves needed more knowledge and understanding about the higher education context for minority women faculty. This was a recurring recommendation to the president and provosts in meetings with them and more content on this has been incorporated into their in-services. At my university, training of department chairs on the importance of inclusiveness was sporadic at best. Some had been in their positions a long time and assumed that junior faculty knew what was required of them. A few women had the impression that the chairs were mentoring their male counterparts informally when they had coffee or played sports with them but most junior women didn't have that same personal time, so they felt excluded from inside information. The MWF network began to provide junior women faculty with more senior mentors who could offered information available within the "good old boy network" to male junior faculty. This was done through a series of promotion and tenure workshops organized, structured, and implemented by minority women faculty for each other.

Initially we collaborated with the provost's office in planning university workshops on the promotion and tenure process, trying to ensure that issues important to minority women faculty would be included. In the last several years however, we've planned our own workshops, exclusively for and by minority women faculty and these have been most fruitful. Although we have not been able to conduct workshops each year depending on time and leadership, those that have taken place have helped junior faculty over their six year period as assistant professors. The MWF membership prioritized topics for the workshop through their listserv, then the more senior members helped to plan and organize the content and logistics for the workshops. Initial topics suggested for the workshop were: preparing manuscripts for publication, writing statements for promotion and tenure packets, external reviewers, teaching evaluations, writing workshops and support groups, defining service and leadership, research support and opportunities, mentoring workshops at the college level, and publishing a MWF survivors' handbook/manual. Members prioritized and decided to incorporate these topics into a series of three workshops that addressed the three areas reviewed for promotion and tenure in all institutions: research, teaching, and service. They decided on a hands-on workshop format instead of panel discussions or speakers because they wanted concrete, meaningful information that could be used in their own personal situation.

The workshop on research dealt primarily with how to write an effective statement and why statements are important. The faculty statement about their research, teaching, and service in promotion and tenure packets is an often overlooked piece of required materials but it is crucial in describing a faculty member's work. It is especially important for minority women faculty whose research may be about issues and questions not generally studied by white male faculty. Unfortunately, many minority women faculty find themselves alone when starting to write this statement and according to some of the group, they didn't realize how important the statement was to their case for promotion and tenure. An effective statement describes not only the accomplishments of the faculty member but clearly states her goals and matches those goals with her accomplishments. It is not just a listing of achievements but an opportunity to convince readers that the faculty member has uniquely accomplished important work that makes a comprehensive, important contribution to an academic field and in many cases, impacts practices outside of the university context. How does one start writing such a statement? What does an effective statement look like? Are there some things that shouldn't go into the statement? What is enough or too much? Copies of effective statements from senior women faculty were made available at the Research workshop so participants could discuss and analyze strengths and see how they could maximize the organization of their own statement. In some cases, candidates brought drafts of their statements for senior faculty to give individual feedback. Some junior faculty who were not yet ready for writing statements followed up later by asking colleagues they met at the workshop to review their statements when they were ready to put materials together. Having contacts to rely on for feedback was an important outcome of this workshop.

The workshop on teaching was conducted at the University Teaching Center by university personnel whose work was specifically to help faculty improve teaching as well as to showcase faculty teaching. These presenters had concrete samples and suggestions for highlighting teaching from all over the university. They provided a teaching portfolio rubric with extensive suggestions for what to include and how to organize teaching records and strengths. For example, *materials from oneself* such as descriptions of steps taken to improve teaching, *materials from others* such as letters from students, colleagues' observations, honors, recognitions, *products of good teaching* including students' success in advanced study in the field, and other items such as curriculum revision and development. They provided samples of faculty statements on teaching philosophies and how to connect teaching with research.

Teaching is becoming a more important and valued area even in research institutions and is often a strength for minority women to showcase. It was also felt that minority women faculty often have heavy and difficult teaching loads whose complexity is not recognized when reviewed for promotion and tenure. For example, one Native American assistant professor's load consisted of teaching courses at a reservation in the state. This outreach to the reservation of course, was something that the faculty member wanted to do and something that gave the university great publicity and good will from the Native American community but it also took an enormous amount of time as the reservation was hours away. On paper, her teaching load looked like any other junior professor, two courses per semester, but when most faculty just walked down the hall or across campus to their classes, she had to drive two hours to reach her class and two hours back to the city. In reviewing her papers, however, her department chair did not acknowledge that the time commitment for her was far more than for others who taught on campus. Further, even though the university was praised for offering university coursework on the reservation, that is, for taking the university to the community, her work in this was not acknowledged when it was time for peer review within her department and college. She absolutely needed to present her teaching record so that the department and college recognized her contribution to the university, a contribution that was unique and valued at every level. This helped to allay the faculty concern that the hours spent commuting could be used for writing which often counted more in her peer evaluation.

The common perception among MWF members that their workloads tended to be heavier in the number of courses and the nature of the courses was not easy to document without formally studying faculty workloads. So, this was another suggestion to the President to investigate along with the perception that students tended to evaluate minority women faculty more harshly than white male faculty. This investigation has not yet taken place but is still being pushed at meetings with university administration. Finally, service is an area where minority women tend to shine. Every university is looking for minorities to be on every committee, and to show that the administration is trying to be "inclusive." Minority women in particular seemed to be asked frequently because they cover gender as well as race/ethnicity. The University does this to cover itself in addressing diversity but sometimes administrators truly want diverse representation on various committees and task forces. Since there are fewer minority women faculty and they are more in demand, individuals tend to be called upon more frequently to serve on these committees and task forces. Minority women then are caught in a dilemma of having to make a no-win choice, of saying no to their chairs when asked to serve or agreeing and getting loaded down with service commitments. To make matters worse, service is not an area that is prized by most institutions of higher education especially Research I institutions.

So, our service workshop focused on how service can and should be cast as leadership, often in areas important to the institution's mission, for example, a university's land grant mission. The value of casting service as leadership in areas important to the mission of the university is something that can change with the university administration but it is still a worthwhile way for minority women to view what they do. Over the years, there have been provosts who value this more than others but the important thing is for the women faculty to value how they contribute and to showcase it.

Since research and publications still reign supreme in higher education, workshop participants sought to find ways to connect service to research and scholarship. For example, how did minority women's service reflect, complement, or extend their research? Workshop participants were encouraged to be strategic in their choice of service commitments so that it reflects or enhances research. This meant looking at committee work through a different lens. Some committees are more important than others when they deal with issues valued by the university. Service as leadership and as an extension of research was also a topic at meetings with the president and provosts. For many minority women this changed the way of thinking about service to thinking about it as something potentially important to stakeholders in the university and relevant to their work as researchers.

Conclusions

An integral aspect of the network that turned out to be critically important is the email listserv which now has fifty members. The group decided early on that we didn't need more meetings, i.e., more "service" so, instead, with our email listserv we keep in touch. We believe the key to success for us has been our focus on getting faculty through the promotion and tenure process, at least for assistant professors. The listserv functions as a discussion forum for minority women when we are prioritizing topics for discussions with the president and provosts. Everyone can post their thoughts and opinions knowing that they will be taken seriously and that they are safe in expressing themselves. It serves as the glue that connects minority women faculty who are spread across campus in all the different colleges. Announcements of events, faculty resources such as grant opportunities, and policies affecting faculty are regularly sent via the listserv but the most fun and in some ways the most important function is the celebration of accomplishments and talents of the members. MWF members are quick to send news when someone receives recognition for a publication, an award, a grant, any milestone in their careers. When members begin to receive email after email congratulating them on an award, publication, and best of all promotion, there is a burst of energy when "toasted" over email. Spring announcements of promotion and tenure especially bring joyous congratulations across the email. This explosion of congratulatory messages flying across the emails is like receiving bouquets of flowers from all sides.

It is difficult to explain or exaggerate the joy, the sense of accomplishment, and satisfaction when someone begins to receive notes of congratulations. There is a sense of security and well being to know that you have colleagues who truly experience joy at your accomplishment. One member's comment summarizes, "We have created our own microclimate of support for women of color on this campus. It is an amazing resource!" Since MWF began meeting, eleven of its members have been promoted to associate with tenure. The only gatherings we do have besides the workshops are the year-end celebrations to celebrate the success of colleagues who are promoted that year!

The mega-strategy offered by MWF is that of organizing yourselves into an effective network. Identify other minority women (or any marginalized group) who feel as you do, and prioritize what is important to you. There are many things minority women feel passionate about but sticking to one focus instead of diluting efforts and energy enabled MWF members to find success in the promotion and tenure process. We learned the importance of planning and strategizing to find and utilize university resources (administrators, faculty teaching centers, etc.) and to make clear what is needed from the university in order to promote success. Sticking together, sharing experiences, and celebrating each others' victories enabled network members to create a warm and supportive climate on campus. As new minority women are hired a new cycle begins. We have added promotion to full professorship to our priority list as we continue to bring together the elements of the perfect storm.

Keep on Pushing

Earning Tenure at a Predominantly White Liberal Arts College While Staying True to My African American Culture

D‍WAYNE M‍ACK

As a first-generation African American college graduate who entered the white dominated professoriate, the road to tenure and promotion to associate professor of American history has been a challenging, but rewarding experience. You would think growing up in one of the worst housing projects in Brooklyn, New York, and receiving a substandard primary and secondary education had ill-prepared me to face the rigors of the academy. Despite the vicious cycle of poverty that once surrounded me, I refused to allow it to define me. My humble beginnings inspired me to push through adversity — to make a way out of no way — to keep on pushing. Such a fierce drive contributed to my earning tenure and promotion within five years of my hire date at a small liberal arts college in the upper South — indeed hundreds of miles from the fast, hustle-bustle and hectic pace of New York.

Because of my current success in the academy, I thought it was important to share with other faculty of color how I was able to successfully complete the tenure and promotion process from assistant to associate professor. I am sure whether you are African American, Asian American, Native American, any other hyphenated American of color or even female, my story will resonate with you to some degree. Over the years I have witnessed other faculty of color agonize over the tenure process; some have legitimate concerns and others, less worthy of contemplation. Many of these men and women stress over situations that are sometimes trivial and often irrelevant.

Occasionally, I am able to reassure these individuals the tenure and promotion process is not too complicated and that they too can remain true to their racial and ethnic identities. Instead of spending an inordinate amount of time finding ways to pacify a committee (which can often be an exercise in futility), I advocate faculty of color first tend to their own personal, professional and psychological needs. As underrepresented faculty, we can maneuver successfully through the tenure process without compromising our integrity or cultural needs. You should execute a tenure and promotion strategy that promotes not only your institution's mission, but your own professional agenda as well.

Despite the fact that this essay is written from the perspective of an African American male historian at a small liberal arts college, I encourage those at much larger institutions to incorporate or at least consider employing some of my strategies in their efforts to achieve tenure and promotion.

Classroom and Campus Challenges

Although there is a growing consensus in America that we live in a post-racial society because Barack Obama, a biracial black man was elected to the presidency, race continues to matter. Do you remember the furor that erupted in 2009 over President Obama's first scheduled address to America's youth? Conservative legislators and political pundits encouraged millions of Americans to boycott the president's speech to America's children on September 8 of that year by either removing their children from classrooms, keeping them out of school that day, or demanding school administrators pull the plug on the speech in classrooms across the nation (McKinley and Dillon, 2009, p. 1).

This same resistance to the authority of African Americans and other non-white intellectuals is also commonplace in college classrooms. No matter how much faculty of color attempt to conform and adhere to Eurocentric American professional standards and classroom etiquette, a number of white students and colleagues alike view minority educators simply as "token hires." This marginalization of minority faculty to a large degree impedes the learning process. Students who have been raised in environments where people of color have been seen as inferior and in other negative manners are often not receptive to lectures that are infused with racialized oriented content. As a result, students and faculty alike, avoid taboo discussions about race in the classroom.

For a historian whose scholarship is heavily focused on race, it is impossible to avoid such subjects. My lectures on slavery and Jim Crow, for example, often cast me in the eyes of many white and even some disillusioned black coeds as a person of color who harbors a deep hatred of white America or that I am "playing the race card." As it relates to the latter, I remind my students that the entire deck is racially loaded. Some of my teaching evaluations can attest to this observation. Students have anonymously labeled me a "racist" and said, "he hates white people and blames them for everything." Despite their misdirected frustration with the course content, I searched for creative ways to educate a generation of young people (the Millennials) who have a limited conceptualization of race in America. In fact, I teach in a state that the Southern Poverty Law Center has given a grade of "F" for its inability to teach the civil rights movement, "one the most defining events of U.S. history" ("SPLC Study," 2011, p. 4).

Conscious of this dynamic, I sometimes soften the truth in the classroom with light humor. Usually on the first day of class I inform my students the course content will not include race because it is ill-related to history. Needless to say they are confronted from day one with race-based content. Even when it comes to issues of equity among faculty, the viewpoints of minority faculty are often not valued in departmental meetings. We have minimal, if any voice in the decision making process and our voices are often muted, if not outright silenced. In the academy, minority faculty are somehow expected to "go along with the program" and some of this hostility is filtered from the top down. Negative white attitudes regarding the academic and cultural capital of faculty of color trickle down from administrators and colleagues into the classroom.

By the way of illustration, right around the time I authored this essay, a white professor at my institution wrote a disparaging Tweet about his African American student (Blackford, 2011). His racially insensitive remarks violated the trust of the student(s), and compromised the student's identity through a social media site because the now infamous "Tweet" went viral. Notwithstanding, some students and faculty refused to define the professor's actions as racially motivated.

In this climate of institutional denial, it is almost impossible to persuade uncompromising forces to accept one's lived expertise and intellectual contributions. Underrepresented faculty, however, must remain steadfast in this often unfriendly environment. It can often seem that others devalue our presence on campus. In navigating our professional career paths, and cultivating our creative talents both on and off campus, I suggest being *proactive* in our roles as faculty of color can often improve our chances for earning tenure and promotion.

Adopting a Tenure Approach

In the process of compiling a tenure dossier, many tenure track faculty have followed the advice offered in *The Teaching Portfolio: A Practical Guide to Improved Performance and Promotion/Tenure Decisions* by teaching specialist Peter Seldin (2010). In this informative guide, Seldin provides excerpts from successful teaching portfolios across different disciplines. Most exemplars feature academics at research institutions and larger universities where "publish or perish" is part of the institutional culture.

Missing from Seldin's text were portfolios featuring African American history, or discussions about teaching courses with racial content. Also missing were discussions about the differences in seeking tenure for African Americans or other faculty of color vs. their white counterparts. In spite of this race neutral approach, I still followed Seldin's traditional guide for earning tenure, but also incorporated my personal teaching practices as a member of an "endangered cohort" (Warde, 2009 p. 495) in a predominantly white professoriate. I approached earning tenure through an African American lens, developing a unique plan focusing on campus and community compatibility, preventing isolation, and community engagement. These strategies enabled me to earn tenure and promotion.

Determining Campus Compatibility

After a long arduous journey to earn a B.A., at a small predominantly white southern Christian college, and M.A. at a historically black university in the South, and finally a Ph.D. in history from a PAC 12 institution in the state of Washington, I was excited to be on my way to a career in higher education. Before I entered the professoriate, like so many newly minted Ph.D.s, I considered the "ivory towers" to be a democracy with liberal thinkers within its walls (Diggs, Wade, Estrada and Galindo, 2009; Jones, 2004). This disillusioned poor soul, however, quickly learned an institution also contains rigid spaces where there exists "subtle acts of racism" (Diggs et al., 313) or unpatrolled acts of "microaggressions" (Diggs et al., 313; Soloranzano, Ceja and Yosso, 2000). Institutional racism is real for faculty of color. It is important to understand an institution is a microcosm of the real world — there are safe, nurturing cocoons as well as hostile spaces designed to crush careers and stifle professional dissent. As underrepresented faculty, we must search out nurturing environments that are conducive in allowing us to further our careers without sacrificing our integrity in the process.

That being said, faculty of color (like all faculty for that matter), are really looking for an institution where they are compatible both professionally and socially. Sometimes finding such compatibility is a challenge because we operate in an unparalleled campus universe, with its own unique set of social dynamics. As members of a minority group, many of us need to feel a sense of connection to an institution because it promotes self efficacy. Our goal is to become effective as educators and scholars.

For this reason, after I earned my doctorate I diligently searched for an institutional environment where my intended goals could reach fruition. Although central Kentucky is not a major destination for African Americans in higher education, I accepted my first and only tenure track position at Berea College in the fall of 2003 because part of its long and pioneering history included serving economically-challenged black students and this complemented my research agenda.

Since I am a historian engaged in research on the black experience, I understood the college could contribute to my professional and social growth; a place where I could hone my teaching and research skills. There are several intangibles related to whether we are embraced by our peers. As underrepresented faculty, on the road to tenure, many of us search for ways to fit within a dominant Euro American academic environment. For the most part, we become part of "subcultures" (Trower, 2009, p. 43) within our departments or institutions. Sometimes we must ignore the negative attitudes of colleagues directed toward us or the poor record of an institution as it relates to promoting diversity. Many of us have already dealt with this racial dynamic in graduate school and for junior faculty, the tenure-track experience is no different. Despite the lack of campus collegiality, we share a responsibility to make a "way out of no way" in adjusting to our professional and personal environments.

When deciding on compatibility, I encourage faculty of color to consider the demographics of the surrounding campus. Part of becoming compatible with the institution's culture and mission also includes feeling acceptance on campus and its surrounding community. Not all campuses are child friendly. At that time my wife and I had three children and a few years later we had another child. I remember during my interview most faculty assured us that children were indeed welcomed. After living in the largely racially homogenous state of Washington for six years, I longed to raise our children in a more racially diverse community and surround them in a community where they could attend an African American church and cultural programs. Berea became that fit for me. Regardless of religious denomination, spirituality can be a significant part of the tenure process. The spiritual growth and fellowship with other Christians provided both a balance in my life as well as a social outlet. Tenure became more attainable because an accommodating campus and proximity to black churches afforded me the opportunity to practice and express my spirituality.

As an African American parent and historian, I also understood the importance of maintaining professional and personal life balance. I wanted to avoid "cultural taxation," (Padilla, 1994, p. 26), the unrewarded "expectation" that faculty of color will spend limitless hours on campus engaging students of color, serving on committees to fulfill diversity quotas, and of course serving as the campus community's spokesperson for their respective racial or ethnic cohort (Stanley, 2006;

Thompson, 2008). I made it clear to my colleagues not only am I career focused, but as an African American male it was important for me to balance my professional, personal, and parental responsibilities. Sharing childrearing responsibilities with my spouse is a part of my life I value. I refused to allow the occasional excesses of campus socialization to prohibit me from carrying out my personal agenda. As faculty of color we must avoid overlapping our professional and private responsibilities, however, it is sometimes easier said than done. When we establish our professional limits with our institutions, it can alleviate some academic strain. Creating this balance allows us to have time away from the office and prevents us from being consumed by stressful and unreasonable workloads. Although I am aware of the backlash women of color experience in the academy for their obligations to their families, clearly recognizing and establishing boundaries and personal parameters will serve as a compass in defining campus and community compatibility and set the tone for engagement with an institution's culture. This allows us to stay true to ourselves, respect our own priorities, and avoid burnout.

Preventing Social Isolation

Besides finding a niche, faculty of color often suffer from professional isolation within their respective departments, programs and divisions. At times, we experience isolation campus wide. For the most part, we should never expect a colleague to embrace us in a traditional sense with open arms. Isolation is real and at times I could relate to the main character, Dan Freeman, in the book *The Spook Who Sat by the Door.* I was the only faculty of color in a white dominated department where I had access to some inside information, but a racial gulf existed between me and my colleagues. The "outsider within" (Collins, 1986) syndrome is also real for faculty of color. We are placed in awkward and artificial spaces as the "first" of our race or ethnic group to be hired for a tenure track position. For this reason, we enter departments with a predominantly white and male faculty who have no desire to mentor faculty of color.

For me, mentorship was one of the most important keys to earning tenure and promotion. Most faculty of color expect traditional forms of mentoring. In fact, faculty of color perhaps rarely receive "mentoring, inside information or valuable connections and networks" (Moody, 2004, p. 18; qtd. in Stanley, 2006, p. 14). If we fail to become proactive and fail to seek out professional relationships, they will not materialize. White colleagues may or may not see a need to mentor faculty of color the same way they reach out and groom other white junior faculty. I know it did not happen for me and most likely it will not happen for most faculty of color. Nonetheless, it is to our advantage to initiate a collegial relationship with non-minority faculty. This form of "cross mentoring" (Thompson, 2008, p. 53; Stanley, 2006) is important to our survival in the academy.

As the only African American faculty member in my department, from day one, I expected to experience some degree of social isolation. Some white colleagues in my department, however, who were part of the baby boomer generation briefly reached out to me. As they approached retirement, I am sure they were secure in their own skin. For me and other faculty of color, some mentoring occurs in nontraditional spaces like water fountains and in front of the coffee pot in the faculty lounge.

Wherever a faculty member offers supplemental advice in a peripheral setting for advancing your career, this is part of the informal mentoring process. For example, one such unconventional mentoring session occurred my first semester at Berea. During a brief encounter in the faculty lounge an older colleague mentioned to me our college's participation in the Selma to Montgomery March in 1965. He had come across this information while conducting research in our institution's library for his manuscript on another topic. He suggested I conduct some preliminary research on Berea's role in this historic event. Since I recognized this form of mentoring, I followed through with his advice and discovered a treasure trove of primary resources related to the college's role in the historic march. In fact, this local research project would provide a better work and life balance by not interfering with my off campus family responsibilities. My acceptance of my colleague's informal approach to mentoring also contributed to my producing peer reviewed articles on the subject. These publications also brought significant positive publicity to the college, highlighting the institution's mission of racial inclusivity. One of the articles was also included in the freshmen composition reader in our institution's general studies program. The use of the article brought me out of social isolation because now some faculty embraced me through my research. Needless to say, my research agenda and success was later articulated in my tenure portfolio.

Finding faculty of color to serve as a mentor can also be a challenge in itself. On most campuses minority faculty are spread throughout campus. They are sometimes socially disconnected from other minority faculty and for reasons of white colleague backlash — some avoid such opportunities to form nurturing relationships. African American mentorship has been important to my success. It has trained me how to navigate the political waters of my institution. Similar to the way slave parents nurtured and shared survival skills with their children on the plantation or the parents of young activists reminding them of Jim Crow etiquette, black faculty, my mentors of color have taught me how to survive, politically. For example, an African American colleague frequently mentored me about the racial politics of the institution. He also identified those whites on campus who were allies of diversity. I must also recognize the role my mentor served as a local gatekeeper. He introduced me to members of the black community off campus and this contributed to longtime residents easily embracing me. In fact, it was through him we found a home church. Without his support and guidance becoming accepted in the black community and attaining tenure and promotion would have been much more difficult.

My experience is a classic example of why I encourage underrepresented faculty to network with supportive senior faculty of color and be open to informal mentoring from white colleagues. I have experienced the best of both worlds where faculty of color and non-minority faculty have served as mentors. Effective mentoring rescues us from social isolation on and off campus. More importantly, mentoring also contributes to our professional development as we progress as educators in the classroom and as scholars.

Engage in Service Learning

After experiencing some teaching success during my first two years, my probationary review recommended I reflect on my teaching, so I reassessed my approach. I wanted to improve student learning and thus positively influence teaching evaluations. After participating in a Spring 2006 service-learning seminar directed by a colleague, I learned how to incorporate experiential learning through community engagement. The seminar motivated me to teach a civil rights course that included a service-learning component.

Service learning is perhaps an effective way to promote faculty efficacy. This teaching tool serves as a vehicle for faculty of color to become ambassadors of their institutions and actively engage community partners in meaningful projects. All institutions have a rich historical connection to their surrounding community. Since my institution's history stretches from slavery through the civil rights movement, I had a significant amount of local resources at my disposal. However, because of my co-parenting responsibilities I could not travel abroad or even go to other states like my colleagues to facilitate student learning. For this reason, community engagement provided me the best experiential opportunity to engage my students outside of the classroom. Similar to my earlier research projects on Berea's role in the civil rights movement, service learning provided me with another homespun research topic.

As a faculty member of color and budding scholar, I approached service-learning as a holistic way to cultivate a meaningful relationship between the campus and the black community and as a pedagogical tool to transform student learning. I developed this course to train upper division history majors how to conduct oral histories in order to document the history of a local black church. For the service-learning project I collaborated with African American elders in my own place of worship. This church has served as a pillar of the surrounding African American Appalachian community for over a century. The focal point of the service-learning assignment were video interviews and photograph sessions with church members who reflected on their experiences of civil rights activism and the role that the church played in sustaining the community. As promising historians, my students became active learners engaged in their own learning process. Besides reading historical scholarship, they also researched, interpreted, and authored history (Mendel-Reyes and Mack, 2009). Faculty of color can pursue similar projects. The church could be the synagogue, temple or mosque. Instead of collaborating with a place of worship, the community partner could be a secular organization. Establishing partnerships with local nursing homes, shelters, or after school programs are just among a few ideal and potentially rewarding possibilities for minority faculty and community partners.

Service learning renewed the relationship between large segments of the black community and the college. More importantly, this course encouraged successful student learning and student evaluations of my teaching. By conducting and transcribing interviews, writing a term paper based on their research, and producing a documentary, students became active learners in the purest sense. As authors of history, their learning experience became completely transformed. The course also served as inspiration for a published essay collaboration with a senior colleague (Mendel-Reyes et al.).

Moreover, the service learning course served as my contribution to interracial coeducation at Berea College, reflected in post term teaching evaluations. Students wrote: "He taught me to think outside of the box and be more flexible" and "This course furthered my goals in being a historian." In essence, service learning served as a platform to bridge a gap between the college and community; built trust between me and the community; created a sense of purpose for me in the black community; encouraged preferred student learning outcomes; and raised my teaching evaluations. For faculty of color, community engagement is one of the innovative ways to earn positive feedback from students, thus improving your chances of tenure and promotion. This creative teaching approach produced several desired outcomes that influenced my tenure and promotion granting committee.

Recommendations for Tenure Track Faculty of Color

- Determine your compatibility on and off campus
- Avoid professional isolation by being proactive and developing professional relationships with your colleagues
- Recognize conventional and unconventional forms of cross mentoring
- Build meaningful relationships with senior faculty of color
- Engage in community service-learning to build a bridge between your institution and the community

- Remain true to your cultural identity on and off campus
- Collaborate with colleagues on research and publication projects

These creative strategies served to place me on the pathway to earning tenure and promotion at a small liberal arts college. During my journey, I was able to remain true to my African American identity and passion for black history. Because of my urban grooming, surviving at a majority white institution was easy to accomplish. I offer these recommendations as a corrective to already informative works that have not yet incorporated my field and cultural background into their tenure and promotion texts. My insights should also offer a unique and personal view into the tenure process at an institution where the focus is on teaching first and scholarship second. There is indeed an intrinsic reward in doing your work well and caring about its quality. I continue to seek new ways to improve my teaching and research. Most of my strategies are student-centered and promote student learning resulting in favorable student feedback. The feedback was especially helpful as I reflected on my teaching maturity in preparing my tenure portfolio. In essence I found creative ways to bridge a gap between campus and community which ensured I maintained a professional/life balance while remaining true to my African American heritage. In developing our academic identities, no one size fits all. Within institutional structures, it is clear we need creative, alternative strategies to find our niches in order to "keep on pushing" toward tenure and promotion.

REFERENCES

Blackford, L. (December 9, 2011) Berea college professor apologizes for racially charged tweet. *Lexington Herald Leader.* Retrieved January 27, 2012, from http://www.kentucky.com/2011/12/08/1987528/berea-college-professor apologizes.html#storylink=rss#storylink=cpy.
Collins, P. H. (1986, October–December). Learning from the outside within: The sociological significance of black feminist thought. *Social Problems* (33), 14–32.
Diggs, G., D. Wade, D. Estrada, and R. Galindo (2009). Smiling faces and colored spaces: The experiences of faculty of color pursuing tenure in the academy. *Urban Review*, 41, 312–333.
Jones, L. (2004). Forward. In D. Cleveland (Ed.), *A long way to go: Conversations about race by African American faculty and graduate students.* New York: Peter Lang.

McKinley, J. C., and S. Dillon (September 3, 2009). Obama's plan for school talk ignites a revolt. *New York Times.* p. 1.

Mendel-Reyes, M., and D. Mack (2009). We'll better understand it better by and by: Three dimensional approach to teaching race through community engagement. In S. Evans, C. Taylor, M. Dunlap, and D. Miller (eds.), *African Americans and community engagement in higher education* (pp. 135–147), State University of New York Press.

Moody, J. (2004). *Faculty diversity: Problems and solutions.* New York: Taylor and Francis.

Padilla, A. M. (1994). Ethnic minority scholars, research, and mentoring: Current and future issues. *Educational Researcher, 23* (4), 26.

Seldin, P. (2010). *The teaching portfolio: A practical guide to improved performance and promotion/tenure decisions* (4th ed.). San Francisco: Jossey-Bass.

Solorazano, D., M. Ceja, and T. Yosso (2000). Critical race theory, racial micro-aggressions, and campus racial climate: The experiences of African American college students. *Journal of Negro Education,* 69 (1–2), 60–73.

Stanley, C. A. (2006). An overview of the literature. In C.A. Stanley (Ed.), *Faculty of color: Teaching in predominantly white colleges and universities.* Bolton, MA: Anker.

SPLC study: More than half of states fail at teaching civil rights movement (Winter 2011). Southern Poverty Law Center Report.

Thompson, C. Q. (2008). Recruitment, retention, and mentoring faculty of color: The chronicle continues. *New Directions for Higher Education,* 143, 47–54.

Trower, C. A. (2009) Toward a greater understanding of the tenure track for minorities. *Change: The Magazine of Higher Learning, 41* (5), 38–45.

Warde, B. (2009). The road to tenure: Narratives of African American male tenured professors. *Journal of African American Studies,* 13, 494–508.

Multiple Voices
Same Song

JACQUELINE B. TEMPLE, YER J. THAO, *and* SAMUEL D. HENRY

Introduction

"No one's self is ready-made; each of us has to create a self by choice of action, action in the world. Such action, if it is meaningful, must be informed by critical reflection, because the one who is submerged, who cannot see, is likely to be caught in stasis, unable to move. But the kinds of choices that are necessary can only be made when there are openings, when appropriate social conditions exist. So the matter of the diminution of self is two-pronged; it demands reflective thinking on the part of individuals, and it demands social change."

— Maxine Greene, *Landscapes of Learning*, p. 18

One place that higher education frequently goes to when examining who may join the exclusive club is: "this person does not fit." It is the message spoken aloud for student-applicants, for faculty screening committees, and for making promotion and tenure decisions. No surprise, it is a message frequently directed to faculty of color. Of course, there are many underlying assumptions as subtext to this message. Subtexts like: (1) "I fit, but you don't"; (2) "I am the arbiter of who fits, and based on something I know, I have decided that you do not belong"; (3) "you have to fit our [my] expectations to make a contribution to our organization"; and (4) "your work is of a lesser quality." There is frequently a presumption directed toward the faculty of color that they are expected to respond to this very serious accusatory statement, and expected to provide a plea or counter some argument in their waning defense. The statement might be delivered as if it is a court indictment. Color or race differentials are very rarely acknowledged in this exchange; status is the focus of the interaction — as if race/ethnicity/linguistic background/color plays no role in this status equation. It is almost always presumed that "not fitting" should be remediated, but of course, if it is our color and ethnic status, not fitting can't be changed. At times, this scenario is manifested as a plea to "just go away." At other times it appears as the construction of an indictment or the common-sense confirmation of clearly apparent inferiority.

For some faculty of color, these messages are often-repeated statements about a perceived accent or use of the English language. Often these messages are accompanied by references to vague or specific student complaints about language, about the "overuse" of narrative illustrations during teaching, differing teaching styles, and student reports of confrontation because they were asked to respond to questions during class. Or it may be coupled with the most insidious complaint: "I just can't understand him/her." Like many of the messages given to faculty of color there is frequently a similar message along gender lines about fit, and in our experiences women faculty of color often get multiple versions of the don't fit message. So, what can the faculty member do?

The following stories or personal narratives are provocative and will assist fellow faculty in understanding the inner and outer struggles we encountered in negotiating our research and teaching expertise at predominantly white institutions (Osajama, 2009). While our stories are drawn from different points of view, and at different period of times, the lessons learned are uniquely interrelated.

My Journey as an Inclusive Educator: Jacqueline B. Temple

Growing up in the South was my first-hand encounter with racial exclusionary discrimination under Jim Crow laws of segregation. Then, as a secondary special educator, I was very perplexed hearing complaints such as "I wasn't trained to teach those kids," from my general education colleagues. Their prejudiced resistance and lack of knowledge in teaching for inclusive diversity in addition to my own encounters with discrimination led me to advocate for *all* children who have been relegated to the isolated margins of schools and society. These are the cornerstones of my life-long journey in being an activist for those who are subjected to educational and social injustice.

This essay reflects my experience and my efforts to transform inclusive education into a practice of freedom (hooks, 1994). Therefore, for me personally and professionally, inclusion is a matter of uprooting racism in schools and society. This is influenced by my commitment to equity and diversity issues, and my belief that all children possess gifts and talents, and the inherent right to belong. To this end, in 1997 I joined the faculty in the Curriculum and Instruction Department with expertise in the inclusion of students with special needs into the educational arena. Then, in 2001–02, I was awarded a Fulbright Scholarship to lecture and conduct research in Inclusion/School Integration at the University of Jyväskylä, Jyväskylä, Finland. So in the fall of 2001, I joined the Special Education Department in Finland. In both institutions, my belief of inclusion as being the vehicle for improving race relations has been my solace. In fostering the Fulbright's mission of mutual understanding, I've worked to alter my students' thinking from merely the technical aspect of teaching, to an interrogation of critical issues of institutional racism and educational inequities in schools and society, and their implications for teachers and higher education.

Through my multi-cultural heritage of Native American, African and European American, my teaching and scholarship examines discriminatory and prejudicial policies and practices in the education of students from diverse cultures and ethnicities—with/out disabilities, and the role teacher education plays in preparing educators to teach for inclusive diversity. In the U.S. and Finland I lived the contextualized experience of being a multi-cultural individual in a fairly mono-cultural environment. In both environments, my students and I investigated what teacher educators should do in preparing pre-service candidates for teaching students who have been systematically excluded from the educational arena? We discuss the productive tensions that arise when examining privilege as well as the policies and procedures that promote equity. In the process, we engage in critical dialogue where the diversity of thinking and of sharing the multiplicities of languages, cultures, races, and ethnicities are imbedded throughout all of my courses. Hence, the knowledge and the voices of diverse scholars of color are moved from the margins to the center of the canon. Needless to say, this style of teaching as, Nieto (2002) states, frightens many people because it challenges their cherished notions that education is based on equality and fair play. In Finland, while I might have been *the other* because of my race, I was not treated as the *institutionalized other*. There, the students (and colleagues) were receptive, critical thinkers, curious, and provocative learners. In contrast, three weeks into my journey at my home institution, I felt like the sacrificial lamb when a colleague from a different department asked: "How is your department treating you? Your department has problems ... they don't know how to treat and respond to faculty of color. They recruit them — but they have no idea of how to maintain them!" Later I was warned about being too out spoken! I was told: "You'll never get tenure, if you keep talking like that!" I quickly realized that my values, knowledge, integrity, and experiences were in conflict with those of the academy. Having to negotiate my identity and being under constant surveillance was isolating and demoralizing. I agonized about whether I was too vocal in expressing my ideas about inclusivity as a catalyst for change. I questioned: Who could be trusted and were they really trustworthy? Will my scholarship be respected, affirmed, and validated?

Critical Learning Encounters

Living abroad helped me to contextualize my social and professional encounters with colleagues and students. The Fulbright experience affirmed the support of a broader community beyond the academy that made it possible for me to maintain my sanity and sense of purpose while creating new intentional visions of education that transgress racial and social injustice. I realize that these encounters were/are critical learning experiences for me *owning my truth* and in having the courage to transform fixed stereotypes and boundaries in the academy. They

143

provided a deeper meaning to the categories of events and contexts in which they occurred. Throughout my years, I've come to feel a sense of renewal and grounding. Despite the institution's focus on social justice and ethnic diversity, I've learned that in many instances, having a professor of color and being exposed to critical content that pushes students to think deeply and consciously about education in relationship to the practice of freedom (hooks, 1994) is a first for students from the dominant culture. Recognizing this has fueled my commitment in being intentionally inclusive and in fostering global understanding through people-people diplomacy. As a result, I've held firm to the adage that "educators must work to establish a community that does not demand the suppression of one's identity in order to become socialized to abstract norms. We must support the development of organizations in which inter-relatedness and concern for others is central" (Tierney and Bensimon, 1996, p. 16).

My journey has been a constructivist endeavor that entailed learning how to challenge the ever present subtle boundaries and thrive in an isolating and chilly cultural environment. I am an associate professor and the director of the International Teacher Education Licensure Program. Achieving tenure was an affirmation and renewal of my two unreconciled strivings: my integrity and my passion. In my courses I am compelled to embed my history, values, and experiences, for these are integral to my cultural and professional identity and have kept me from being torn asunder (Du Bois, 1897). My scholarship continues to investigate biased policies and curricula which re-inscribe systems of dominance while investigating new ways of teaching for inclusive diversity. In response to: What can faculty of color do? My advice is to speak your truth and situate your voice through your content, pedagogy, and your scholarship. Know that you do have a viable message to deliver even if the immediate situation does not allow for such. But, pick your battles wisely. Locate mentors and be a mentor. Focus on your research and scholarship agenda. Be true to yourself and know that you are not alone. Understand that doubt and fear will occur from time to time, but never sacrifice your integrity, because you are genuine. Last, establish a network of community support both inside and outside of your department and the academy.

Journey as a Pioneer Professor: Yer J. Thao

The journey to become a college professor as a person of color was an unusual experience for me. I felt like I was reborn into the university culture that reflects only white American culture (coming from a Mong culture). Mong is an ethnic minority hill-tribe from Laos. I literally had to learn how to live, survive, and function in an institution that is unfamiliar about faculty of colors' struggle like mine. The challenging experience I had was to understand my identity and culture. I felt isolated, lonely, and afraid because I did not know my colleagues and administrators nor did they know who I was in order to build trust and have mutual support. Another obstacle I had was not being sure about how white students would view my intellectual skills. Most of the time, I felt like they thought that I was not qualified to be their professor. This led to encounters in many situations where I experienced hostility and resistance with students or at meetings with faculty. I constantly reminded myself that my teaching must reflect the course purpose and allow students to explore the profession through different learning experiences. Whatever words I said at meetings were carefully chosen so they wouldn't offend my colleagues. I am always well prepared for classroom teaching and staff meetings because I do not want to be criticized for not being knowledgeable. McKay (2001) describes how faculty of color should aim for best practices in the classroom: "They should always be organized, prepared, and meet classes on time; they must not be condescending to students, but challenge them and entertain high expectations for them" (p. 57).

I came from a culture that has a strong kinship system. I was taught to be respectful to all people. The way I understand people comes from my cultural perspective, which is to be listener, always willing to care for others, and doing my best to show my support for others. I hope that with this expectation people would do the same to me in return. This interpretation was quickly revised because I learned that as a faculty of color I am expected to do more and get little in return. Sometimes, I felt overwhelmed asking why do I have to be the one who has to know everything? It was tokenism. I felt I was walking on a very thin line where I was vulnerable. I was not sure whom to trust. It is remarkable to me that I'm still here and found myself to be a professor of higher education, even while I struggle everyday to find my identity and place of boundary.

My experience as a faculty member of color at my home institution has been unusual. You probably would not know how I feel or understand my experience unless you lived and worked in an environment that pays little attention to minorities' concerns. You need to be in my shoes in order to know exactly what I mean. Often, I consult with other minority colleagues to build my strength and seek personal and professional advice.

Although it is a great opportunity and honor to have a tenured position at my current institution, I sometimes wonder where am I? I am not comfortable sharing my personal struggles with colleagues who have no commitment to supporting faculty of color. Therefore, I often feel like I am a foreigner in my campus community. I decided to focus inwardly by remaining silent and acting mellow so I can be safe, rather than act radically. In my view, faculty and students from all cultural backgrounds should build upon their past understandings and gain new information through interaction with others and culture exchanges. I seek, in all my efforts, to involve faculty and students in understanding who I am and encourage them to apply their new insights to their own experience.

My passion is teaching and doing research in cultures, as part of cross-cultural, multicultural, and multilingual education, it has always been my focus point in connection with other social issues that dominate culture within the systems of power. Darder explains the relationship between culture and power:

> In order to understand the relationship between culture and power we must also comprehend the dynamics that exist between what is considered truth (or knowledge) and power. It is this relationship that has seldom been questioned with respect to its effect on schooling and its control of what constitutes knowledge in American schools [Darder, 1993, p. 27].

The importance of language and cultural diversity often is hidden from students in the dominant group, as well as from minority students who find no expressions in the formal school curriculum of their own cultural perspectives. This process of training is especially harmful to students who have experienced social oppression. Without proper guidance to help these students understand the causes of their oppressive experience, a self-limiting view of victimization could easily take root in these already violated minds. My teaching provides a sociocultural space not only to reveal silenced and marginalized voices from different frames of cultural reference, but also to recognize how they interconnect and interplay with the dominant voice in the power hierarchies in local and global contexts. Therefore, creating a student-centered and inclusive learning environment is crucial for teachers to understand how human diversity and commonality is important to our own lives. The inclusive learning process encourages us to see the interconnection between diverse human experiences and not engage in stereotyping. Multicultural education scholars and researchers state that if students become more literate in culture and language they will reduce their nonreflective nationalist and ethnocentric behaviors (Banks, 2006; Banks, 2003). Sleeter and Grant (2003) have added that teaching multicultural education will help students to eliminate prejudice, foster positive human relations, and promote harmony among racial groups.

The mission of the Graduate School of Education at my home institution is "Preparing professionals to meet our diverse communities' lifelong educational needs," and the mission of my home institution is "To enhance the intellectual, social, cultural and economic qualities of urban life." These preambles have inspired me to continue my scholarship in teaching, research and community outreach efforts. However, I am not sure whether this university is totally committed to invest and support faculty and students like me.

As a faculty of color, teaching theories that address cultural oppression and education for social justice to mainstream students can be challenging. Regardless of how well I teach the course, there are some students who cannot relate to my personal experience and to the cultural and linguistic pedagogy; as a result, they sometimes feel disconnected. This has, unfortunately, contributed to lower ratings on my teaching evaluations. For example, the students who have not developed a philosophical and sociological sense of justice were sometimes unable to connect personally with course topics. Students may then have disliked the way I structured my class, viewed my class assignments as difficult, and

147

displayed inappropriate behaviors in class. bell hooks (1994) stated, "I have found that students from upper and middle-class backgrounds are disturbed if heated exchange takes place in the classroom. Many of them equate loud talk or interruptions with rude and threatening behavior" (p. 187). They may have resisted the information and materials I use in teaching. As a professor of color, I learned through observation that a longer time is required by non-minority students and faculty to accept the knowledge presented in class or at meeting. After reading through this narrative, I am hopeful that you will understand my personal struggle as a faculty of color.

My Journey as a Public Intellectual and Educator: Samuel D. Henry

My song is sung with multi-layered harmonies and complex rhythms; my song is about diversity. Sung and danced with deep roots and pulsations from Africa, North America, the Caribbean and Western Europe; this music is part gospel, funk, blues, fusion jazz, rock and roll, and a dab of classical cello—it doesn't explain itself and it is never sung alone. Likewise, my academic career captures streams of experience that flow from my biography: culture contact, teaching, service and leadership in multiple communities. The experiences cross a spectrum of civic responsibility: from developing curriculum that resists oppression, to mentoring and coaching graduate students, to bridging human chasms with dialogue, liberation and common interest.

I was born into a tri-ethnic black family in post–World War II Washington. D.C., and was educated in the D.C. public schools. I was groomed to leadership in this extended family aware of our heritage and histories of former slaves, the black Caribbean experience, and Native People's reservations. I was also shaped in my local Washington community with diverse mentors: black, white, Jewish, Creole, the black Pentecostal church, and by our proximity to the national government. Our daily family dinner conversation incubated an understanding of international politics and domestic economics, blended with family news and insights on neighborhood issues. Without a TV in the house due to Mom's insistence on first attaining high school level reading, us kids, openly discussed and became more familiar with the work of congressional leaders and Supreme Court justices, and the subjects of Marcus Garvey, race riots during World War II, and issues of the capital of the free world, where Negroes couldn't hope to buy a house. It was the fifties. We talked about tomatoes thrown at Vice President Richard Nixon on his visit to Venezuela, the Red Scare, Sputnik, and school desegregation, as well as the style and delivery of last Sunday's preacher from exotic north Texas—a black man named Cortez. Then, too, at home there were evidences of my mother's professional connections and her successes in science and in higher education, and my father's love of community, religious fidelity, and his passion for helping those down and out—all parts of my formative education. After 10 years in post–*Brown v. Board of Education* in D.C. public schools and witnessing white flight, I graduated from high school, then from historically black, D.C. Teachers College, along the way performing military service with the D.C. Army National Guard, including serving during urban riots after the assassination of Martin Luther King, Jr. I lived my first twenty years in the cauldron of social change bubbling underneath a societal blanket of dire and life-smothering oppression feeding my later academic role in questioning the status quo.

After college, I taught English and social studies in local D.C. schools, then, in Binghamton, New York. Next, I attended Columbia University Teachers College, in New York City, earning first a master's degree in curriculum development and then a doctorate in urban education, completing a dissertation field study that examined the schooling experience as the confluence between culture(s), curricula, organizational behavior and students' selfhood. I lived in Morningside Heights next to campus, close to Harlem, beside the in-migration of the Dominican Republic and benefited from ethnically diverse mentors who nurtured and helped sustained my thirst for the broadest kind of liberation in education. I would not have survived without them, or my childhood "fellas" who regularly visited from D.C., and the West Indian wing of my family that literally and spiritually fed me.

After grad school, my first faculty position was at the University of Massachusetts, Amherst, directing an urban education program, and participating in the Boston School Desegregation project. There, again,

I witnessed the ugliness of racial hatred and prejudice in our country; yet, in counterpoint, I also was permanently "adopted" and given emotional shelter by a family of white New England German heritage immigrant farmers. Then, I moved back to New York City to direct the federal regional (New York, New Jersey, Virgin Islands and Puerto Rico) school desegregation assistance center at Columbia University. This immersion in serving equity through academic work in community was followed by several leadership positions: staffer for a university president, a social sciences and an education associate dean, and as a university assistant vice president. Over time working in California, I was able to play a role in transforming a university to a more diverse place — so I know it can be done.

Moving to Oregon in the early 1990s, I led a multi-agency school reform organization, and served in faculty positions with the school of education and the college of urban and public affairs at a regional university. I maintained a public life as a diversity consultant, and worked with political campaigns and civic organizations. Recently, I completed six years as the chair of the statewide children's commission, and nominated by the governor, I now serve on the state education school board. I have tried to be an academic who is a fully participatory public intellectual — to me that has meant connecting the ivy walls to the marble halls.

In thirty years of higher education, and through experiences at five different predominantly white institutions, I have found several myths wrapped in pervasive and demoralizing messages served up to faculty of color. These messages should be recognized and countered in order to help our colleagues survive in higher education in the United States. If wisdom is built up in conversations and interactions as Freire (1970), has suggested, the goal here is to speak humane care to and with each other, such that certain truths become visible. Sonia Nieto suggests that "The major difference between individual discrimination and institutional discrimination is the wielding of power, because it is primarily through the power of people who control the institutions such as schools that oppressive policies and practices are reinforced and legitimized" (1996, p. 37). These messages are conveyed because of power or the perception of power. In surviving in academia, power must be dealt with, messages purposefully re-constructed, and the insertion of freedom declared. Adhering to negative messages is to be a participant in your own slow strangulation and spiritual death.

In sum, along this journey, my music has been made more beautiful by relationships: parents, family, mentors, students and colleagues, which I strive to support at the university. I have been loved and supported, or as my treasured mentor, Dwayne Huebner, said: "they helped listen me into clarity." My hope is that singing my song will help in raising and countering toxic university messages that faculty of color hear, and assist us in entering into dialogue with others where opportunities are made for faculty of color to persist and prosper throughout academia. Such that I have had, the poetry of the world becomes the syncopation of your song.

Conclusion

Many faculty of color are experiencing the same song that is heard through and from different voices and perspectives. Hence, the authors' stories clearly revealed that in order for faculty of color to be successful we must seek mentors outside his/her department and at different universities to prevent academic death and scholarly demise. In addition, we must be the supportive network for each other and create an authentic community of difference among colleagues from a range of racial and ethnic groups and academic backgrounds. This collaboration is needed for allies to develop collegial and respectful relationships across institutional departments so that we can be affirmed for our rich talents and valuable contributions. American colleges and universities need to be committed to efforts to support faculty of color at all levels by creating an environment where faculty of color are empowered to share their stories, maintain strong self-identity and have a trusted collegiality rather than hostility. Whicker, Kronenfeld and Strickland (1993) reminded us a decade ago that dissimilar backgrounds of faculty members reduce the possibility of having collegiality, friendship, and informal information dissemination. Where white faculty and faculty of color colleagues have common cultural backgrounds and values and accept each other's differences as the norm of American higher education, those institutions can achieve a trusted atmosphere for all. This essay is one piece of many unheard stories that are connected by common threads of *colorful* faculties, who've made the journey toward tenure and other successes.

REFERENCES

Banks, A. J. (2006). *Cultural diversity and education: Foundations, curriculum, and teaching.* New York: Pearson.

Banks, J., and M. A. Banks (1993). *Multicultural education: Issues and perspectives.* Boston: Allyn & Bacon.

Darder, A. (1993). *Culture and power in the classroom.* Westport, CT: Bergin & Garvey.

Du Bois, W. E. B. (1897, August). Strivings of the negro people. *The Atlantic Monthly* (08). Retrieved on January 2, 2012, from http://www.theatlantic.com/.

Freire, P. (1970). *Pedagogy of the Oppressed.* New York: Seagate.

Greene, Maxine. (1978). *Landscapes of learning.* New York: Teachers College Press.

hooks, b. (1994). *Teaching to transgress: Education as the practice of freedom.* New York: Routledge.

McKay, N. Y. (2001). Minority faculty in [mainstream White] academia. In A. Leigh DeNeef and Craufurd D. Goodwin (eds.). *The academic's handbook* (pp. 51–79). Durham, NC: Duke University Press.

Nieto, S. (1996). *Affirming diversity: The sociopolitical context of multicultural education,* 2d edition. White Plains, NY: Longman.

Nieto, S. (2002). *Language, culture, and teaching: Critical perspectives for a new century.* Mahaw, NJ: Lawrence Erlbaum Associates.

Osajima, K. (2009, May/June). Telling our stories to one another: Narrative is a powerful tool for linking faculty, especially faculty of color. *Academe, 3*(95), 28–29.

Sleeter, C., and C. Grant (2003). *Making choices for multicultural education: Five approaches to race, class, and gender.* New York: John Wiley & Sons.

Stevens, D. D., and J. E. Cooper (2002). *Tenure in the sacred grove: Issues and strategies for women and minority faculty.* Albany: State University of New York Press.

Tierney, W. G., and E. M. Bensimon (1996). *Promotion and tenure: Community and socialization in academe.* Albany: State University of New York Press.

Whicker, M. L., J. J. Kronenfeld, and R. A. Strickland (1993). *Getting tenure.* Newbury Park, CA: SAGE.

Bearing Children on the Tenure Track
Survival Strategies from the Trenches
MICHELLE MADSEN CAMACHO

The late Gloria Anzaldua, renowned Chicana author and cultural theorist, coined the term *mundo zurdo* to describe the spaces of contradiction, tension and ambiguity in which we reside (Anzaluda, 1987). Writing powerfully from the margins of feminism, Anzaldua and other scholars of color gave such spaces a voice, naming the liminal spaces of academia, and describing the territorial cross-roads and complex borderlands where scholars of color embody "difference" and signify a social "other." Anzaldua theorized the rifts within feminism, the splits within Chicano Studies, and the flaws and faults of a society that produce rigid categories and prevent a number of allegiances in multiple worlds. Within academia, women of color as mothers and scholars inhabit such compound identities. Surprisingly, very little scholarly literature has considered how we navigate our way within the ivory tower.

The narrow space for academic women of color as mothers is riddled with cultural contradictions. While some departments have pivotal faculty who are welcoming and supportive, others are chilly environments populated with few faculty that have young children or faculty who are less openly supportive. Maushart argues that as mothers we wear "masks of motherhood" that keep us silent so as to not appear unprofessional (2000). Douglas and Michaels contend that societal "mommy myths"

153

romanticize standards of motherhood resulting in a denial of difficulties (2004). These cultural standards produce stigmas for those who transgress socially constructed ideas of idealized motherhood. Within academia mothers sometimes hide within the mommy closet, unsure of how motherhood might impact their social capital. Mothers, especially of young children, are a minority group among university faculty. Typically institutional support structures fall short of addressing not only the micro-level challenges faced by academic mothers, but also the macro-level policies that fail to consider this group. At micro and macro levels, stereotypes intersect based on organizing principles of race, gender, class, ability, sexuality, and across all the aforementioned factors: motherhood.

Motherhood and race are salient status characteristics that when combined produce biased perceptions of competence, leading to lower salaries and diminished opportunities for advancement. In a famous experiment led by social researchers at Cornell University, scholars found that simply adding the phrase "has a two-year-old child" created perceptions of a less competent job candidate compared with an otherwise equal candidate not presented as having a child (Correll, Benard and Paik, 2007). The researchers found that race compounded the effect. Additionally, mothers suffered a substantial wage penalty compared with fathers and non-mothers (Correll, Benard and Paik, 2007).

Race operates together with motherhood to produce status expectations in which several academic tensions compete. Outside academia, cultural norms produce the expectation that ideal mothers should always be available for their children and willing to harmoniously intertwine their career demands with their child-rearing practices. This motherhood norm clashes with widely-held assumptions that the ideal teacher/ scholar publishes abundantly, produces innovative pedagogical advances, attends university functions at any hour, and commits selflessly to service work. Within academia, faculty of color often do not receive recognition for their "hidden workload" involving commitments that white faculty are not expected to carry (Kolodny, 2000). Our hidden workload involves serving a plethora of diversity committees, offering critical perspectives on marginalization and inclusion, recruiting and mentoring faculty and students of color, and redirecting weak institutional policies related to diversity and cultural competence. Academic women of color are also more likely to be sought out by students who want to discuss their experiences of racism or sexual harassment and by students experiencing unplanned pregnancies or those who have young children. The myriad of these efforts takes time, and often, these contributions are invisible to and thus undervalued by faculty peers and administration.

The intersection of racialized and mothering stereotypes combines cognitive biases, in-group preferences and cultural prejudices that discriminate against scholars in academia (cf. Tomaskovic-Devey and Stainback, 2007). The effect is subtle discrimination, both entrenched and invisible in organizational structures, that even works against progressive policies. Women who take advantage of flexible family-leave policies, for example, may be stigmatized as less committed to the craft of research. Worse, if work-family policies are not in place and women of color attempt to argue for them, they may be viewed as demanding of special privileges. Raising awareness about the needs related to work-family policies may have negative material effects on women because of societal stereotypes that suggest only "supermoms" can manage both. Therefore taking advantage of special policies may make motherhood status highly salient, with a net negative effect (Correll, et al., 2007).

Additionally, women of color who are mothers must beware of stereotype threats (Steele, 1997). Stereotype threat theory would suggest that academic women of color who are mothers have anxieties that their behaviors will conform to prevailing stereotypes; this, in turn, causes an interpellation of ideologies that further relegates mother-scholars of color to the margins. "Reconciling the competing urgencies of family and work are particularly difficult in situations where a woman is a racially gendered token or solo subject" (Segura, 2003, p. 33).

Historically, men as fathers have fared differently than women. In the past, employers legally paid fathers a "family wage" that was higher to accommodate their breadwinner role. While women suffer a motherhood penalty, men enjoy a fatherhood premium — research on men's wages, backed by robust empirical findings in labor economics, suggests that fathers have a tremendous financial advantage in labor market outcomes (Correll, et al., 2007).

On the tenure track, while men and women with small children share many similar challenges, mothers in academia face different obstacles. For academic men, having children is normative and actually increases time to tenure (Mason and Goulden, 2004). For women by contrast, bearing children on the tenure track is much less common; NSF data indicates a spike in fertility post-tenure (Mason and Goulden, 2004). This suggests that among tenure-track women who wish to bear children, factors encourage them to delay childbearing.

Although the traditional Latino script presents motherhood as a gendered standard, Denise Segura's qualitative interviews with Chicana professors revealed that some choose not to become mothers and reject the normalized cultural motherhood script (2003). One interviewee said, "I'm not a mother and I can't understand all this mother crap that Mexicans have. You know, this worship-the-mother crap'" (Segura, 2003, p. 42). Other Chicana academics "expressed great anguish over their inability to meet the cultural expectations of mothering" (Segura, 2003, p. 42). There is a lack of discussion about these issues and for the most part, these voices are few and mostly silent on this topic in the academy.

While women are earning Ph.D.s at the same rates as men in the social sciences and humanities, institutional factors and workplace structures are not always accommodating to women with children. Women with children are at odds with earning tenure, since biological clocks and career clocks overlap inconveniently. Having an "early baby," (that is, having a baby within five years of receiving a Ph.D.) has been called, "the kiss of death" because women academics who have "early babies" are nearly 30 percent less likely to get a tenure-track position than women without children (Mason and Goulden, 2002, p. 26). Women with Ph.D.s who have early babies are much less likely than others to make it to the ranks of full tenured professor. At the most secure, tenured levels, married men with children dominate the pie not women. Since these patterns are specific to academe, what this means is that there are several social and cultural factors related to institutional climate that affect women's identities as mothers.

Survival Strategies from the Trenches

I learned several informal lessons about how to manage my own identity as a mother and scholar. I bore three children, held two postdoctoral fellowships and embarked on the tenure-track within five years of completing the Ph.D. My three children fall into the category of "early babies"; at one point I had three children under age five while an assistant professor. Below I share my personal narrative as a method of "autoethnography" (Chang, 2008; Ellis and Bochner, 2000) — a reflexive account of my own experience situated within a cultural segment of academia (cf. Flores-Niemann, 1999).

I am an academic misfit because I am the first in my extended working class family to attend college, and few of my Ph.D. colleagues share this background. Half of my family emigrated from Bolivia and worked here in the service industry, and the other half is working class white (and resides in a mobile home trailer park). I grew up with my divorced mother and Spanish was my first language. In this single-parent household my sister and I were latch-key kids. Today some might call our neighborhood "bad" because all of our windows had bars on them, there was graffiti in the alley down the street, and prostitutes worked Harbor Boulevard, half a block from my home. I mention all of this because it informed my academic life and had a profound effect on the types of research questions I am drawn to and the manner in which I inhabit my social position as an academic.

At my own campus not long ago, in a public forum, a faculty member told our former dean that our campus still used the AAUP's 1940s policy on pregnancy and that our campus should adopt the new 2002 policy. He countered that such initiative should come from the faculty. I raised my hand and pointed out that perhaps it would be helpful to have administrative leadership since there was not a swell of demand. The dean conceded that it was a minority issue: "you just don't see too many pregnant professors." In this example we see that the responsibility of forging parent-relevant policy within academia belongs to those who want to hold the door open for others. It is not widely recognized that the challenging path of parenting while publishing may benefit from systematic institutional attention.

As an academic mother I've given quite a bit of thought to managing my own identity, since I have always been hyperaware of my relative minority status in the elite club of academia. For the most part I've learned to live in "the mommy closet," a space where a candid discussion about the pains of pregnancy, the wondrous miracle of birthing, the toils of breast-feeding, the complexity of adoption or infertility and the pitfalls of childcare are not commonplace discussions. The institutional discourse around these translates into a negative terminology emphasizing "stopping, leaving and missing" with phrases such as "stopping the tenure clock" "taking leave" "missing work because of sick children." Far less frequently are the solutions framed positively with phrasing that values the work of care-givers. Many campuses lack systematic policies that celebrate work/life balance with family friendly policies such as part-time tenure tracks. There are still very few structures that enable minority mothers to thrive within academia and maintain a balanced life. In this essay I share five survival strategies that I adopted while bearing children on the tenure track.

Institutional Fit Matters

My first year on the job market, I made a few mistakes. The first big misstep was when I was scheduled for a job interview in a male-dominated Chicano Studies program which at that time had never in its very long history had a female chair. At the time, I had a four month old baby that I was nursing. None of my mentors had counseled me about juggling job interviews with mothering (which is not surprising given that they were all men). I asked the female search-committee chairperson to please provide a window of time so that I could express my breast milk. (When a nursing baby is away from the mother for several hours, the mother's breasts will become absolutely engorged, which means they get very full with milk and sore and lumpy and most likely they will start to leak, not an ideal scenario for a job interview). I needed to make sure I had a few breaks during my full-day visit, which was jam packed with back-to-back interviews leading to my job talk. This is not a typical request. My biggest error, however, was mistakenly assuming the hiring committee would be enchanted with hiring a new scholar who was also a new mother. Without much reflection on how this might affect my job prospect, I freely answered questions about my current position and the excitement of simultaneously being a new parent and new postdoctoral fellow. I didn't get the job. I hadn't read the research indicating that applicants who disclose motherhood status fare poorly compared with non-mothering women (Correll et al., 2007)

Eight months later, at my next tenure-track job interview, I happened to be four months pregnant. I did not reveal my exciting news. I wore a suit that camouflaged my protruding waistline. In the state of California it is technically illegal to be asked about these issues, and so I made no mention of the fact that I had a baby at home and one on the way. This time, I got the job.

The position was a small, private liberal arts university where the teaching load was three courses per semester and the publication requirements were lower than I had been trained to expect at a top-tier research university. For me it was a good fit. Grading papers at home could easily endure far more multiple interruptions than writing. A liberal arts college where teaching was privileged seemed more accommodating and flexible. So my first lesson was: institution matters.

Actively Work Against Stereotype Threat

The theory of "stereotype threat" applies to the case of mother/ academics of color. The theory suggests that, at a micro-level, negative ideas about work performance will be internalized and effectuated. The everyday practices of raising a child powerfully and irreversibly reshape our identities and also affect how we are perceived. Applied in this case, the theory of stereotype threat suggests that, without concerted effort and agency, academic mothers are at risk. To combat this retrograde perception academic mothers need an underground support network.

I'll never forget the advice I received from two highly esteemed colleagues who are very well-respected women of color in academia. Both are mothers. They took me out to lunch and cautioned me not to share my mothering pitfalls with my non-parent colleagues. In no unclear terms they emphasized: "if you have to attend a parent/teacher conference for your children, or take them to the doctor for an emergency, never tell your colleagues! You will be perceived," they warned me, "as less professional, in spite of how accommodating your colleagues may appear." They suggested that instead, I should say, "I have an off campus appointment." This different language, they proposed, would cast me in terms that every non-parent can relate to. At first I refused to believe them, because this language forced me even more deeply into the mommy closet and I felt that I needed to change the culture by being outspoken. And of course, several departments are wonderfully supportive in spite of the salient characteristics of motherhood and race. Nevertheless, how to manage motherhood as an identity must be carefully considered based on departmental climate.

Clearly there is much that needs to change institutionally to prevent stigmatization of mother-academics. In 2006, for example, an article in the *Chronicle of Higher Education* documented the case of a woman at Oklahoma State University whose contract was not renewed because three people complained about her nursing in public, and the chair informed her that the university's lawyer asserted that her office could not be used as a daycare center and, further, that her personal choice in bearing children was not the responsibility of the department (Wilson, 2006). In other words, although our profession may appear to be more flexible than others, such incidents remind us that we are still expected to maintain distinct boundaries. It is important not to assume that all members of our campus community will support our juggling efforts. With tenure comes a responsibility to work to change the campus climate, to push for pro-parent policies, and to work towards de-stigmatizing parental care-giving.

Be Strategic with Publications

Many of us do not receive mentorship about the process of publishing. While I am very grateful to my mentors, I received conflicting advice. "Don't publish too early." "Publish in top tier journals, not in edited book volumes." "Don't theorize your personal experience; it will be too much like a confessional." I found the advice somewhat crippling. In order to be true to our academic identities and publish abundantly, it is important to understand the tenure process at our own institutions, listen to the wisdom of reliable mentors, and ultimately trust our gut instincts in the process of finding our academic voices and writing truth to power. The process of getting published requires confidence and a willingness to take risks. As Wendy Belcher (2009) suggests, successful academic writers persist despite rejection and successful academic writers pursue their passions.

In my case, I found that publishing about my challenges in teaching and my classroom innovations still counted as publications. Theorizing pedagogy can be one strategy for faculty with heavy teaching loads who want to persist in spite of having less research time. Deadlines can also serve as extrinsic motivators. Using a web search one can find calls-for-papers from special issues of journals requesting submissions. Belcher's brilliant path-breaking tome titled, "Writing your Journal Article in Twelve Weeks" encourages similar tips and should be essential reading for all junior faculty and those working to get on the tenure track.

Finally, while co-authorship is more common in some fields than in others, writing with another colleague can be an essential tactic to maintaining scholarly productivity. If you pursue co-authorship opportunities, ensure that your collaborator has a track record of publishing and meeting deadlines. Co-writing research grant proposals is also a worthy investment of time if your research team members have had some previous experience with success.

Enlist a Mentor and Find External Support

Do not fall prey to the sentimental moralism associated with mothering and the idea that the only way our children will be successful is if we strive for perfection. From home-cooking meals to flawlessly holding it all together, the mythical supermom haunts us as an imaginary heroic role. One of my undergraduate students, whose mother is a very successful tenured professor, told me that she grew up on take-out food. Many successful academic women take similar shortcuts and actively critique the media trap that idealizes a model of perfect mothering. As women of color we have persevered in spite of many obstacles. We have unique time management skills and effective organizational capacities; we are talented and competent. A supportive mentor will provide hope and encouragement when we feel our spirit is breaking, and can make all the difference in affirming the value of our work and the importance of work/life balance. One such mentor reassured me, "We are all juggling glass balls and rubber balls. The rubber balls you can drop and it won't matter. I've dropped some, even lost some. As long as the glass ones are still in the air everything will be okay." Another counseled me to schedule an imaginary meeting for myself every week, to literally block out the time on my calendar, and to use this time slot for something that brings me joy.

The data show two compelling trends, one apparent and one surprising. The obvious one is that a supportive partner makes an enormous difference in success rates for women on the tenure track. The surprising finding is that single mothers achieve tenure at higher rates than non-single mothers. What this suggests is that an unsupportive partner is the weakest link. If this situation pertains to you, and the "double shift" becomes unmanageable, enlist help, even if it means running an economic deficit for a short time.

Use Micro-Strategies

According to Mary Ann Mason (former Dean of UC Berkeley and author of many articles and books on the effect of family formation on the careers of women), the data indicate that women who "take off as little time as possible" are most successful (2004). This means not stopping the tenure clock, which is an arguable topic. This idea begs the question, how can we publish, bear children and have a balanced life? I suggest if you have the time available to take, and can afford to, take it.

A very prolific writer once told me that he has written all of his books from 4 to 5 A.M., using just one hour per day. I tried it. I adapted my writing routine to the early morning hours, from 5 to 7 A.M.. This works for me because at this hour everyone is still sleeping and I am neither exhausted nor hungry; it is too early to make phone calls, too quiet to do chores or laundry, and email productivity is still slow. While I was never an early riser, this strategy allowed me to have a little bit of peace at a beautiful time of day when I can sip my coffee and create abundantly. Belcher's book on publishing proposes several strategies for paying attention to writing strategies and creating a writing plan tailored to one's own style (2010). The key is sustained and systematic effort, a little each day, while turning off the nasty-critical voice in your head and allowing yourself the freedom to express your ideas before editing them.

Conclusion

In sum, I have two concluding thoughts. In my first draft of this essay I concluded with the question of "is it worth it?" I felt compelled to end on a happy note considering this essay is full of depressing statistics and anecdotes. I cited a lovely quote from the *Chronicle of Higher Education*, in an article called, "Does having children offer any advantage to an academic's professional career?" It read:

> Having children is an act of great hope, an affirmation that no matter how chaotic and tragic the world seems to be, it is still worth living in. ... That we trust our children to do even better than we [have]. And isn't that why we teach? Isn't every act of walking into the classroom or library, fundamentally, an affirmation of our belief that things could be a little better? I think it is, which is why having children and being an academic can go together. Every act of hope supports and enhances other hopeful acts, and while it isn't necessary to have kids to be a good academic, to have them can be a further expression of, and commitment to, the same impulse that drove us to the academe in the first place [Sayers, 2007, p. C3].

But as a Latina academic with roots in urban poverty, in the academic world I inhabit what Anzaldua calls the "mundo zurdo"—in Spanish this is something like "backwards world." What I take from Anzaldua's framing is that my presence in academia represents a rejection of the status quo on a daily basis. I embody the messiness of human social life, and I practice an epistemology of contradiction, tension and ambiguity. Like the liminal territory of Anzaldua's *nepantla*, I stand at a crossroads, embracing my roots as a social "Other," and continue to occupy that Othered space in the academy as a mother/scholar. What is needed in academia is a redefinition of work, one that de-genders caring and instead views it as a social good rather than an "accommodation" to a disability (pregnancy). We need systematic anti-racist and anti-sexist policies that promote our intellectual health. Beyond my consolation in sharing my voice in this essay, I have a social responsibility to build bridges with other parents/faculty of color, to forge a collective community among us, and most importantly, to find new ways of challenging the rigidity of mothering in academia.

REFERENCES

Anzaldua, G. (1987). *Borderlands/la frontera: The new mestiza.* San Francisco: Aunt Lute.

Belcher, W. L. (2009). *Writing your journal article in twelve weeks: A guide to academic publishing success.* Thousand Oaks, CA: Sage.

Chang, H. (2008). *Autoethnography as method.* Walnut Creek, CA: Left Coast.

Correll, S. J., S. Benard, and I. Paik (2007). Getting a job: Is there a motherhood penalty? *American Journal of Sociology, 112* (5), 1297–1338.

Douglas, S., and M. Michaels (2004). *The mommy myth: The idealization of motherhood and how it has undermined all women.* New York: Free Press.

Ellis, C., A. P. Bochner (2000). Autoethnography, personal narrative, reflexivity: researcher as subject. In N. Denzin and Y. Lincoln (eds.), *Handbook of qualitative research* (pp. 733–768). Thousand Oaks, CA: Sage.

Flores Niemann, Y. (1999). The making of a token: A case study of stereotype threat, stigma, racism, and tokenism in academe. *Frontiers: A Journal of Women Studies, 20* (1), 111–134.

Kolodny, A. (2000). Raising standards while lowering anxieties: Rethinking the promotion and tenure process. In S. Lim and M. Herrera-Sobek (eds.), *Power, race, and gender in academe* (pp. 83–111). New York: Modern Language Association.

Mason, M., and M. Goulden (2002). Do babies matter? *Academe, 88* (6), 21–28. Retrieved from Academic Search Premier database.

Mason, M., and M. Goulden (2004). Do babies matter (part II)? *Academe, 90* (6), 10–15. Retrieved from Academic Search Premier database.

Maushart, S. (2000). *Mask of motherhood: How becoming a mother changes our lives and why we never talk about it.* New York: Penguin.

Sayers, R. [pseudonym]. (December 18, 2007). The kid question. *Chronicle of Higher Education,* p. C3.

Segura, D. A. (2003). Navigating between two worlds: The labyrinth of Chicana intellectual production in the academy. *Journal of Black Studies, 34,* 28–51.

Steele, C. M. (1997). A threat in the air: How stereotypes shape intellectual identity and performance. *American Psychologist. 52* (6), 613–29.

Tomaskovic-Devey, D., and K. Stainback (2007). Discrimination and desegregation: Equal opportunity progress in U.S. private sector workplaces since the Civil Rights Act. *The Annals of the American Academy of Political and Social Science, 609* (1), 49–84.

Wilson, R. (April 7, 2006). Baby trouble at Oklahoma state. *Chronicle of Higher Education.*

The Path to Promotion
to Full Professor

ELWOOD D. WATSON

Several days later I received my letter from the president's office. I took the letter from my campus mailbox, walked down to my office, unlocked the door, tentatively walked in with apprehension, closed the door, slowly sat down at my desk, said a brief prayer and opened the envelope. The letter informed me that my application for promotion to full professor had been reviewed and that he (the president) was pleased to announce that he had approved my request and was forwarding his recommendation to the Board of Regents for approval. Upon reading these words I let out a loud scream!
— Elwood D. Watson, May 2008

For a number of faculty members, once they earn and receive tenure, the journey has been completed; or at least that is what they tend to believe. In reality, only half of the battle has been won. While earning tenure and promotion to associate professor indeed represents a significant accomplishment — there is still one more task to complete — promotion to full professor.

Faculty who desire to achieve the highest academic rank in the academy must acclimate themselves to the formal and subtle mechanisms associated with academic success. These include: (1) acquainting oneself with the promotion process; (2) continuing to focus intensely on research; (3) maintaining collegiality as much as possible; and (4) continuing to cultivate and earn the support and respect of influential people. In my situation, a combination of covert and overt factors became barriers in my effort to secure a promotion.

Acquainting Yourself with the Promotion Process

As someone who was officially promoted to the rank of full professor in August 2008, I am well aware of the various dynamics and obstacles that confront scholars who wish to achieve such a rank. In the summer of 2002, I was granted tenure and promotion to the rank of associate professor by the Tennessee Board of Regents. Needless to say, I was pleased with the outcome, although truthfully, I was fairly confident that I would successfully obtain this goal. During my five years as a junior faculty, my teaching evaluations were excellent. I had published five scholarly articles—one co-authored and four solo pieces. I was the co-recipient of an academic award for one of my articles. I was crucial in revitalizing the graduate program that had been in somewhat of a minor funk when I arrived in 1997. I had successfully directed five theses, which was very unusual for a junior faculty member. I even held two administrative positions during my junior faculty years, one of which was an interim position. No one in my department who had previously gone up for tenure at my stage had my record. In fact, several of my colleagues mentioned this fact to me directly before I submitted my dossier to the department for review.

Continue to Focusing Intensely on Research

Immediately after I had won the first battle (securing tenure and promotion), I began to pursue a *very ambitious* publishing agenda. Indeed, between 2003 and 2007, I successfully published one anthology, two co-edited anthologies, two co-authored articles (one was another award winning article), and had a book length manuscript in the process of being published. This by far exceeded the publishing record anyone else in my department had achieved before obtaining the rank of professor. I felt assured that I would be able to earn promotion to full professor with great success. During the summer of 2004, the Tennessee Board of Regents began to raise the requirements for achieving tenure and promotion. While there were not many specifics in writing, the message was clear. More work (especially research) would be required of any faculty member who desired to be promoted.

Despite such changes, I was still confident that I would achieve promotion without too much difficulty. After all, I still maintained a high level of teaching proficiency. My evaluations were as strong as ever. I continued my active involvement in the department's graduate program by teaching graduate seminars and directing 12 theses during this time period. I shared responsibilities in teaching the department's Honors History Survey Course and continued to sporadically take on administrative positions. I was the associate chair of my department in 2002-2003. Furthermore, I was the recipient of an administrative fellowship during the 2003-2004 academic year and served a second term as interim director of the university's African American Studies Program during the 2004-2005 academic school year. I did not know what more I would need to do to secure the rank of a full professor. I harbored the same level of confidence that I did several years earlier as I went up for promotion to full professor. However, I would be in for a surprise.

While I was not totally oblivious to the dissatisfaction some of my colleagues had with the type of research that I was engaged in, I was not aware of the extent of their resentment until I started the promotion process. Circulating accusations that my work was not "historical" enough, or that "such work would likely not advance me in the profession," or that "my research record was modest" were common. I made the case to several parties, including the tenure and promotion appeals committee (unfortunately I had to go through this process), that my work was indeed relevant to historians as well as to scholars in a number of other disciplines. In fact, I unabashedly discussed the interdisciplinary focus of my work and reinforced how so many of those who were decrying my scholarship were actually the strongest proponents of multidisciplinary research (in spite of the limited amount of published work they had produced).

One of the reasons I was able to publish a significant amount of work was because, in addition to having no family obligations, I was in a town where the opportunities for many social distractions were negligible. This did not mean that I was totally devoid of any social life. Nor did I experience feelings of isolation as so many faculty members of color often do. This could be due to my largely independent spirit. As a relatively young person, I was all too well aware of stories of the solitary scholar who suffered from burnout and other factors that frequently resulted from devoting all his or her time to research and writing. I did not want this to happen to me! I was determined not to make work my entire life and I succeeded in accomplishing that goal (Orey, 2006). During my over a decade long stay here, I have been able to make a number of friends that have kept me grounded in a number of ways. In fact, the local coffeehouses and bookstores have been a haven for me. That being said, I do encourage anyone who, for whatever reason, has the opportunity to pursue a healthy, vigorous research agenda to do so. Such an effort may very well result in personal and professional satisfaction.

Addressing the Issue of Collegiality

For many faculty of color, women, gay and lesbian, disabled and non–Christian faculty alike, the issue of collegiality is one that can be employed to mask racial, gender, physical, sexual preference or religious bias (Stanley, 2006). It has been my experience that in many departments (mine is no exception) a disproportionate amount of power and influence lies with the white majority, more specifically with the white male majority. In his article on racial diversity, Professor R. J. Alger describes the how term collegiality manifests itself:

Collegiality can be a code word for favoring faculty with backgrounds, interests, and political and social perspectives similar to one's own. This vague and subjective criterion can be used against faculty members whose work and ideas challenge traditional orthodoxy in their departments and institutions [Alger, 2000, p. 161].

I could not agree more. In fact, more often than not, terms such as diversity, multiculturalism, collegiality and related ones are bandied about within the halls of academia with apparent enthusiasm, while, at the same time, what such "proponents" of these policies really mean is that they are all for such cultural pluralism, as long as the person of color, different religious beliefs, alternative sexual orientation or disability in question is the sort of person that is willing to accommodate to "our" (white and mostly male) value system, will not offend "our" (white) sensibilities and will not place their comfort before "our" (white) own (Stanley, 2006). The message is clear: anyone who is thinking of "rocking the boat" or even touching it need not apply. Patriarchy and abiding by the status quo are the rules that must be adhered to.

While I am not saying that this is the case in every department, there are nonetheless, a number of departments where such prejudices and attitudes are prevalent, or at the very least, certain faculty members who hold negative views against groups that are different from their own. Fortunately, we have reached a stage in American society where very few people are inclined to overtly express their dislike of other ethnic or marginalized groups; rather, they will resort to other methods to express their discomfort or displeasure with undesired colleagues. Examples, such as "he or she is not a team player," "he or she lacks tactfulness" or "his or her scholarship is a little thin" tend to be the most common charges levied against minority and women faculty members.

Before I became a member of academia, I did not spend too much time thinking about collegiality. Although I had heard a number of faculty members mention the term when I was a doctoral candidate at the University of Maine, I did not see it as applying to me. After all, I considered myself as a person who was friendly and outgoing. I learned about collegiality from my parents, who taught my siblings and me to treat other people with dignity and respect. As far as I am concerned, I have maintained such traits to this very day. Despite such efforts, I was still unable to cultivate congenial relationships with certain members of my department.

Part of the problem resulted in the aforementioned notions of what they saw as "acceptable" collegiality, which meant paternalism on their part and submissiveness on mine. Needless to say, I was not going to subscribe to such a dysfunctional partnership. During my tenure at the institution, I did have occasional conflicts with a few colleagues. Most of the incidents were based on egotistical matters, as opposed to any substantial grievances. I refused to conform to their notion of what a fellow faculty member should be. I was considerably younger than all of my senior faculty colleagues (the person closest in age to me was 17 years my senior) accounted for some of their behavior. This factor, coupled the fact that I would be earning full professor status at the age of 40 (relative young by academia standards), was also a source of contention for a few of my fellow faculty. Some of them did not even land their first tenure track position before they were in their late 30s or in a few cases, mid 40s. It was the intersection of racism and ageism. This was too much for some of them to handle. The situation reached a climax during the summer of 2007. It was at this time that I confronted the then-graduate coordinator about him changing one of my courses without consulting me. Given the fact that he was not the department chair, I found this to be very arrogant and inappropriate. We exchanged several tense, yet professional, e-mails with one another. After about a week, the situation seemed to have settled, or at least I thought so. However, I was in for a surprise.

I was at home one afternoon retrieving my campus messages from my telephone. One of these messages was from my now former department chair requesting that I stop by his office for a chat. As I listened to the depressed tone of his voice, I knew that he did not have good news to share with me. Once we met, he delivered the bad news. The majority of senior faculty had voted against my promotion. The vote was four against, two in support and one abstention. I could see the disappointment on his face. He was well aware of the fact that personal and petty vendettas were the reason for such a decision. Nonetheless, he offered to support my bid for promotion, which greatly pleased me. I told him that I intended to proceed forward and thanked him for his support. He stayed true to his word and voted in support of my promotion.

Rather than getting defensive, I went on the offensive. I contacted a number of people on campus who I had developed strong relationships with and sought their advice on how to handle the dilemma that was facing me. All of them offered constructive, common sense, and in some cases, very innovative suggestions. Each of these individuals urged me to persevere. It is important for me to note that each of the individuals who supported me in my quest for promotion were white. One black professor, who was one of my mentors during my tenure as a junior faculty at the institution, genuinely felt that I should wait another year before I went up for the promotion to full professor. Moreover, this same person was concerned that if I continued to pursue my goals, I would meet an even greater backlash from already disgruntled colleagues and urged to me withdraw my promotion application. I told the faculty member in question that I understood their concern but that I was still forging ahead with my decision.

The fall semester was one of intense anticipation as I patiently waited for the outcome of the college committee decision. I managed to quell such intensity by immersing myself heavily into my courses, directing student theses, continuing my research and attending conferences. I also went out frequently during this semester. Keeping my sanity was of utmost importance.

By December 2007, the college committee had made its decision. The vote was 2–6 against promotion. The college committee praised my teaching and service accomplishments but felt that my research record was "modest." At every other level, the decision and comments echoed those of the previous one. I was a very effective teacher and had accomplished broad and solid service during my tenure at the university, but had yet to "sufficiently distinguish" myself in the area of research. Such a conclusion reflected the internal biases of a conservative context in which minority faculty members are subtly taught to "know their place" within the hierarchy. Though I was disappointed, I immediately began my appeal to the tenure and promotion appeals committee to fight against what I perceived to be a racialized stasis. Rather than at the provost level, however, I decided to appeal at the presidential level.

In early April 2008, I met with the university president and he explained the procedure and what was required and asked me if I understood the process. I made it clear to him that I did and I was willing to go forth. It was also during this meeting that we discussed some of my accomplishments. I know for a fact that several people who I knew over the years had spoken to the president about me in positive terms. It also helped that he was well aware of my contributions to the university and the broader community. About two weeks later, I met with the appeals committee to make my case. In my appeals letter I outlined the following:

- I had a forthcoming monograph that was soon to be published.
- Two of my academic scholarly co-authored articles receive awards.
- I had published seven scholarly articles, all in peer reviewed journals. Three were published in the top ranking journals in their field.
- I had published a groundbreaking work on beauty pageants.
- I published several anthologies that had been well-received.
- I had actively promoted interdisciplinary research in my scholarship.
- My work was referenced by several scholars, including ivy league professors.
- I was frequently approached by publishing companies to review manuscripts.
- I had written a number of op-ed pieces for national newspapers.
- I was quoted by the *New York Times*.
- I had been appointed as a full member of the graduate faculty as an assistant professor.
- I was reappointed as a full member of the graduate faculty in 2005.

I had also made it clear to the appeals committee that several other colleagues were promoted to the rank of full professor without producing any level of serious scholarship, thus the process, as it related to our department, the decision appeared to be arbitrary.

I also outlined my teaching accomplishments:

- At the time, I had successfully directed 19 theses since 2000. That this was far more than any other professor during this time period.
- I had successfully directed two University Honors Theses.
- Virtually all my students went on to pursue attempted Ph.D.s, Law degrees or other professional degrees.
- Several other faculty members in History (and other departments) adopted a number of my teaching strategies and methods.
- I had introduced several new courses, including film to the department curriculum.
- I helped revive the graduate program that was in somewhat of a lull when I arrived in the late 1990s.
- I had actively taught in the University Honors College.
- I had actively lectured in several programs on campus.

I made my case on service as well:

- I had sponsored numerous presentations and special programs at the university that were well received by private citizens, fellow academics, journalists, administrators, public libraries, journalists and the larger community.
- I had served on a number of search committees at the university.
- I was appointed by the university president to serve on the University Ethics Committee in 2005 and was reappointed by him in 2007.
- I had delivered the college address to faculty in the college of Arts & Sciences in 2000.
- I had strengthened our departmental Honors program.
- I had taken my students to several conferences in major cities, such as Chicago, Boston, and Washington, D.C., during my term as advisor to the History Society.
- I had been involved in numerous community activities in the larger community.
- I was asked to serve as an external evaluator for a very promising up-and-coming young scholar at well respected university.

I made my administration accomplishments known as well:

- Twice I served as the interim director of the African American Studies Program
- I served as assistant director of the University Honors Program.
- I served as associate chair of the Department of History for a year.
- I was the recipient of an administrative fellowship.

Unfortunately all my efforts were not enough. A week later, I received an e-mail from the head of the committee that the group had voted against granting me the promotion. A few months later, I found out that the vote was 5–4 against. Moreover, I heard that there had been considerable difficulty for several faculty members in making their decision. Given the fact that one of the detractors from my department was the head of the tenure and promotion appeals search committee, I have my own explanation as to why the meeting in question was supposedly so intense and contentious.

Several days later, I received my letter from the president's office.

I took the letter from my campus mail mailbox, walked down to my office, unlocked the door, tentatively walked in with apprehension, closed the door, slowly sat down at my desk, said a brief prayer and opened the envelope. The letter informed me that my application for promotion to full professor had been reviewed and that he (the president) was pleased to announce that he had approved my request and that he was forwarding his recommendation to the Board of Regents for approval. Upon reading these words, I let out a loud scream! I finally realized that my efforts and those of my supporters had not been in vain. I had lost little battles here and there, but I had won the war!

I emailed the now former president and thanked him for his confidence in my work. I then walked down to the office of then soon to be former department chair with the letter in hand. He read it, shook my hand and we launched into an hour-long talk about what an ordeal it was, yet everything worked out well in the end. I was one happy man that day! Two days later, I saw the president at an end of the year function, where I spoke with him directly and genuinely told him of my appreciation for his decision. He made it clear to me that he had no doubts in making the decision that he did, given the fact that he felt I had more than earned my promotion given my extensive performance at the institution.

Continuing to Cultivate and Earn the Support and Respect of Influential People

When I was promoted to full professor in August 2008, I felt relieved. I felt that I could finally continue to engage in cutting edge teaching and research without having to be concerned about the potential impact on my promotion. By now, any person who has been a part of, or is about to enter academia, has been told about the importance of either having a mentor or being one to up-and-coming junior faculty. I would argue that in the case of obtaining tenure, such guidance is strongly recommended. It would be ideal, and perhaps even preferable, to have a mentor within the institution. However, sometimes, such an arrangement is not possible for faculty members of color, women, gays or lesbians, non–Christians or other minority groups. Therefore, it may be imperative to seek outside mentoring as an alternative. In fact, an ideal situation is to have the opportunity to benefit from both, internal and external mentoring. While having a faculty member of the same ethnic group, gender, religion, sexual orientation etc. may be a preferable, the fact is that this does not always result in the best outcome.

Simply because one has a commonality with another person based on skin pigmentation, class, religion, sexuality, physical impediments etc., does not necessarily imply that one will have any other compatible traits crucial for successful mentorship. To paraphrase the old saying — not everyone who is of your group is of your kind. Despite the assumption that sentiments such as "because he/she is like me, we will understand one another" may be commonplace, this doesn't always translate into reality (Darlington and Durnell, 1996). Even within certain groups, intragroup or nativist conflicts can be deeply rooted. Class, religious, economic, color, caste or regional differences can rear their divisive heads resulting in a less than ideal and, in some cases, a horrendous relationship. Due to this fact, it is advisable for tenure-track and even those tenured faculty members pursuing promotion to full professor to seek mentoring from those who have similar academic, political and career oriented interests.

Academics seeking to gain full professor status need to be aware of the ever-changing dynamics of the culture around them. During the years from a junior to a senior faculty member, which is at a minimum a decade for most faculty, a number of transformations have probably taken place. Certain colleagues have probably retired. Administrative personnel — department chairs, deans, provosts, presidents — who were instrumental in one's inaugural years as a faculty member, may have very well retired, stepped down from their positions or moved on to other institutions. This has certainly been true in my case. I witnessed changes of two department chairs and three deans during the time of my transition from an assistant to a full professor.

Because of the constant revolving environment of academia, it is important that faculty members are able to adapt to such changes. For a faculty member to become stagnant or indifferent once he or she earns tenure can be potentially detrimental for the professor in question. This is especially true for those from traditionally non-represented groups. Stereotypes in academia, as in other institutions, regarding minority groups abound. The often-touted image of college professors as being a liberal group of tenured radicals singing kumbaya and railing against the less enlightened establishment is a major distortion.

While it is true that academia probably does have more liberals than some other institutions, the fact is that much of the liberalism is opportunistic, faux, and based in rhetoric, as opposed to substance. Certainly, there are a number of genuine, progressive people in the academy. However, like any other profession, academia is populated with racists, sexists, homophobes, xenophobes, anti–Semites, and other bigots. Intolerance abounds in academia, like anywhere else; it is perhaps more subtle in some cases, but it is present nonetheless. Therefore, it is important for anyone who intends to pursue a career in this profession to be aware of such a reality.

One of the most important accomplishments that any faculty who wishes to move upward on the ladder of promotion is to earn the respect of influential and well respected faculty and administrators on campus. These are the people who can assist you in achieving success, as well as aiding in your failure. My victory in earning promotion is a case in point. I was fortunate enough to have established a stellar reputation as an effective teacher, excellent researcher and could demonstrate a strong level of service. The university president was well aware of my accomplishments and the contributions I had made to the institution and the larger community. In fact, at times when I saw him on campus, he would stop and speak with me. I was told by several individuals who had considerable contact with him that thought highly of me. This level of respect continued right up until his retirement in January 2012 and I have no doubt it played a significant factor in my being promoted to the rank of full professor (despite several negative recommendations discouraging promotion) at a relatively young age. The president always knew the truth. He may also have been aware of the unfounded resistance that surrounded my application.

I want to make it clear that I am not suggesting that anyone should disregard or ignore people who are not in influential positions, quite to the contrary. One should treat every person with dignity and respect regardless of their station. However, it is important to be aware of the fact that there are specific people who can render a decision that can, in some cases, determine your fate for good or ill. It is also important to be aware that no matter how much you want to achieve and advance in your career that you must maintain your self-respect, integrity and human dignity. No job is worth sacrificing any of these virtues no matter how tempting, financially lucrative or prominent the position or rank may be.

Promotion to the rank of full professor is the highest academic rank one can obtain and it is a great feeling to achieve such an accomplishment. I would be less than honest with you if I did not tell you that I wished that I would have had an easier road in earning it. What reasonable and rational person wouldn't? Nonetheless, my experience made me an even stronger person and it was certainly a great feeling to emerge victorious and on the winning side of a long, drawn out battle. I achieved my promotion the old fashioned way. I earned it!

REFERENCES

Alger, J. (November 23, 2000). How to recruit and promote minority faculty: Start by playing fair. *Black Issues in Higher Education, 17*(20), 160–161.
Darlington, P., and N. Y. Durnell (February 22, 1996). Faculty life 101: A survival guide. (Recruitment & retention: The last word). *Black Issues in Higher Education.*
Orey, B. D. (2006). Teaching and researching: "The politics of race" in a majority white institution. In Christine Stanley (Ed.). *Faculty of Color: Teaching in Predominantly White Colleges and Universities* (pp. 234–246). Bolton, MA: Anker.
Stanley, C. A. (2006). Walking between two cultures: The misunderstood Jamaican woman. In Christine Stanley (Ed.). *Faculty of color: Teaching in predominantly white colleges and universities* (328–343). Bolton, MA: Anker.

Writing an Effective Curriculum Vitae

An Introduction to Presenting and Promoting Your Academic Career

ANGELA M. NELSON

The first curriculum vitae I ever read was my mother's: Dr. Martha Ellen Blanding Spence. She completed her doctorate of musical arts from the University of Southern Mississippi in 1977, one of the first African Americans to do so. My mother was on the faculty of St. Augustine's College in Raleigh, North Carolina, from 1975 until her death in 1980. When she died, I was 16 years old. I found her CV a few years later when I was looking through boxes of her work-related belongings (I told my voice teacher I could probably find sheet music in her things to be used in my lessons). I didn't know what I was looking at but at the top of her CV was the title "Vita." I noticed this "vita" included the birth dates of me and my two brothers, her height, and marital status. I also saw that it listed the recitals she had given. That part was especially interesting to me because I was majoring in music education at Converse College in Spartanburg, South Carolina. I had no idea at that age I would pursue a career as a college professor or that I would need her CV or that it would instruct me in the way that it has over the next ten years of my life.

After I entered the American Culture Studies doctoral program at Bowling Green State University, I realized I would need a CV rather than a résumé. I held on to my mother's CV all those years so I knew what a CV looked like. I soon realized the CV is an academic version of a résumé. I created my first CV in 1988, the first year I entered the doctoral program. It was barely two pages long and I faithfully kept updating it as each year passed. The major purpose for it at that point in my career was to begin documenting my earned degrees, service, teaching, and research experience, publications, presentations, and related activities and experiences. This was important to me because I knew I wanted a faculty position when I completed my doctorate. Although the most significant time I needed my CV was when I applied for a few postdoctoral fellowships during the third year of my doctoral program and again when I applied for jobs when I was nearing the completion of my doctorate. I had no formal training in learning how to create my CV. My CV training was much like what happens in folk tradition where information is usually passed by word of mouth within a small local community. In my case, it was a small academic community that included mentors, dissertation supervisors, and professors. It is important for faculty of color to develop a clear and organized CV because it will be easier for your department and College's promotion and tenure review committees to see and find the information they need to make an effective evaluation of your application.

Over the years, I have learned in order to create and update a CV, as faculty of color we need certain documents that provide factual information about your academic activities. It is best to save and consult various documents so your information is accurate. For research/ scholarship and creative activity: speaking invitation letters (electronic or paper), citations for book reviews, journal articles, books, encyclopedia entries, exhibition catalogs, performance event programs, conference paper acceptances, conference programs (paper or electronic), and grant notification letters are helpful. For teaching, having copies of student numerical ratings of teaching reports, class rosters, syllabi, exams, and other course materials will assist in compiling the teaching section of the CV. For documenting service, journal or book manuscript reviews, invitations to do reviews, committee election and/or appointment letters, publication or broadcast interviews with reporters, and board election and/or appointment letters can be a help. It is best to consult undergraduate and graduate transcripts to provide accurate information regarding your degree areas, majors and minors, and years obtained.

It just so happened that as I was developing my own CV that my husband was training and consulting with others on how to perfect his résumé and to help others develop their own résumés. His passion for résumé-writing inspired my personal quest for learning how to develop good CVs. In April 2003, I gave my first workshop on writing CVs. Researching and preparing for the workshop revealed a lot of information such as what is essential to put in the CV and what should not be documented in a CV. There are seven essential components of the CV: (1) identification and contact information, (2) educational information, (3) academic and/or work experience, (4) teaching activity, (5) research activity, (6) service activity, and (7) miscellaneous activities. These components form the major parts of the CV and are included in a CV template at the end of this essay. The identification and contact information should be located in the first part of the CV and should include: Your name, first and last [do not use middle initials or middle name unless it is normally used by you]; contact address, apartment number; city, state, Zip Code; 1+ area code, contact phone number; and e-mail address.

A personal webpage URL is not necessary on the CV; I doubt any committee member would look at it. In addition, since creating PDFs of documents is more accessible in many colleges and universities today, fax telephone numbers are unnecessary and should not be included. (Note: If your university still uses fax machines for the transmission of certain important documents, then include your academic unit's fax number on your CV.) Regarding your contact address, select your home address or your business address but not both. Today, an e-mail account is necessary and is the primary means of communication in job searches, faculty evaluations, and the basic operating processes in higher education. The second section of the CV, the educational information should list degrees (with commencement honors and specializations), certifications, licensures, accreditations, clearances, registrations, and diplomas. Lists of faculty positions and ranks; post-doctoral fellowships; academic administrative, editorial, or other non-teaching experience; graduate student teaching/research assistantships and fellowships, undergraduate student teaching/research assistantships and fellowships; K–12 teaching; tutoring; and other relevant employment should be in the academic and/or work experience section. The teaching activity section should include introductory, upper division, upper division/graduate and graduate courses taught; student evaluations of teaching (optional); theses and dissertation students; formal academic advising and mentoring; and curriculum development (courses, workshops, educational materials) among other items.

The research, scholarship and creative activity section can include peer-reviewed publications (books, journal articles, book chapters, book reviews, abstracts, reports, multimedia materials), conference papers and lectures; grants, contracts, patents awarded; faculty fellowships; performances, exhibitions; compositions, arrangements, and scores; prizes, product or engineering designs, and patents. The service and citizenship activity section may include service and citizenship within a faculty member's department, division, school, college, and university and in their profession (committees, review panels, leadership positions, consultantships) and community (partnerships with schools, other forms of outreach); and professional development courses and workshops presented.

The CV is a unique, personalized document that can have several types of additional information based on the education and experiences of the person writing it. Therefore, miscellaneous topics can cover a wide range of items. Some of these are administrative and instructional professional development; continuing education experiences (courses, workshops, improvement leaves, post-doctoral training); honors and awards; membership in professional organizations or honor societies; endorsements; study abroad, language competencies; research/creative activity, teaching, and service interests; references/recommendations and placement file.

While the seven components are necessary in a typical CV, there are some types of information which should not be included. This is not the case in all countries in the world but certainly in the United States of America. Rebecca Anthony and Gerald Roe state that "Federal and state guidelines prohibit employers from basing hiring decisions on such characteristics as the applicant's age, sex, race, religion, disability, and national origin" (1998, p. 23). Generally, I believe, as faculty of color we should view this practice as being in our favor. Other types of items or information to refrain from including are your signature; photograph; place of birth; social security number; physical characteristics including gender, height, weight, and eye color (remember my mother's CV); family information including marital status, name and occupation of spouse, and names and ages of children; ethnicity or political affiliation; military service or civic service; and hobbies or personal travel. It would be admissible to provide some of the items related to religion and the military if it is "required" for the position in which you are applying, e.g., position at religious high school, college, or university; military high school or college; military research think-tank, etc.

As I mentioned above, the CV is a personal yet, significant professional document. It is the evidence most readers turn to when first assessing whose application to keep, whose to cut, and assessing whether a probationary faculty member has satisfied their teaching, research, and service responsibilities. Minority faculty and those pursuing faculty positions vary in their beliefs, values, and experiences with regard to creating a CV. Since by-and-large few faculty members and future faculty members have formal training in developing a CV, awareness of and/or judgments concerning moral, ethical, and legal considerations will vary. Some factors I will address are What to Include in the CV; Padding; Inaccuracies; Privacy vs. Public Disclosure; Social Media Technologies; and Your Professional Life. A tenure and promotion candidate of color should carefully consider all suggestions about information you "should" include in your CV.

Incorporate only those suggestions that make sense to you. Balance the opinions of others against your own convictions. YOU, alone, must defend the voracity and content of your CV. There is no such thing as a "bad CV." In other words, a "badly" constructed CV will not cause you to lose a job opportunity or tenure and promotion unless there is a scenario where massive amounts of basic information is omitted from it such as contact information, educational background, etc. Certain types of information may look like "padding." Do not exaggerate your accomplishments. Remove information and activities that are not directly related to teaching, research, and service as defined by your college or university. Refrain from including incidental (although important, necessary activities) such as writing letters of recommendations for colleagues or conducting and writing peer evaluations for colleagues. On the other hand, noting you were on an external review team for a college's 10-year accreditation or an academic unit's program review or that you served as an external reviewer for a candidate's bid for promotion to full professor should be noted. Furthermore, avoid listing hobbies or interests—these can be seen as filler or unnecessary "fluff," and can detract from the overall professional appearance of your CV.

Dates, academic degrees, and experiences are critical to the hiring and tenure and promotion processes. Therefore, information in the CV must be accurate and truthful. The discovery of inaccuracies, untruths, or misrepresentations will usually preclude further consideration of your candidacy. Once hired, the discovery that you have provided false information can be cause for termination. Lying on a CV about work experience, education, or training in order to get a job is fraud, a serious criminal and civil offense. CVs are essentially public, although not official, autobiographical documents; they list your earned degrees and past "public" academic-related experiences and skills. As such, they probably should not be considered to be private, confidential documents. Nevertheless, be cautious about distributing your CV to persons you are unlikely to work with in some type of professional capacity. In addition, know that from a legal perspective, e-mail turns everyone into a "publisher." Therefore, also be cautious about disseminating your CV electronically via the Internet or e-mail. Since all e-mail is recorded and can be produced in court, inaccurate information, for example, in your CV could be problematic if this scenario were played out.

New social media technologies including blogs, personal web sites, and social networking service accounts have the power and potential to positively or negatively impact your job searching efforts or maintain your current position. Social networking services allow users to create a profile for themselves. In most networking sites, users can upload pictures of themselves, create their "profile," and can often be "friends" with other users. Social networks usually have privacy controls that allow the user to choose who can view their profile or contact them, etc. Most social network services are web based and provide a variety of ways for users to interact. Popular social networking services in the United States are Facebook, MySpace, Twitter, and LinkedIn. Below are several issues for underrepresented faculty to consider for reflection in regards to CVs and social media technologies: Should I share confidential information?; What impact could making inappropriate comments about my university have on my career?; What does my university consider to be inappropriate?; What is the availability of certain personal information to my employers?; What will my employer consider to be inappropriate content on my personal blog, web site, or social networking site?; Should I list my blog or web site on my CV?; What is the potential impact of my writing a job search blog?

I have given a basic overview of the purpose and components of the CV and some of the ethical and legal factors to consider. Now, I will discuss the writing and formatting of the basic CV. (Note: A CV template follows this essay.) The organization of the CV is important. Attention should be given to how you use fonts, font sizes, white space, bolding, block text, header placement and graphics (Formo and Reed, 1999, p. 19). You want the appropriate tenure and promotion committees to find the information they need when evaluating your application therefore, CVs must have categories or section headings (see examples below). Section headings and categories are functional and thematic. This means the heading or category used specifically and clearly shows what type of information will follow in it. Within each category and heading, information should be listed in reverse chronological order, e.g., 2005, 2004, 2002, etc. One key heading to refrain from using is "Curriculum Vitae" or "Vitae"; do not list it on your CV. Overall, categories and section headings should be brief and limited to the following titles:

Categories and Section Headings

academic preparation	comprehensive areas
academic training	master's project
degrees	thesis
dissertation	
dissertation title	professional competencies and
dissertation topic	special skills

184

course highlights
experience highlights
related professional experience
research appointments
research experience

academic accomplishments
professional achievements
career achievements
career highlights
background
research overview
administrative experience
education highlights
proficiencies
areas of knowledge
areas of expertise
areas of experience
areas of concentration in graduate study
graduate fieldwork
graduate practicums
specialized training
internships
teaching/research assistant-
ship

teaching interests
academic interests
research interests
educational interests

postdoctoral experience(s)
professional interests
professional experience
professional overview

professional background
academic appointments

convention addresses
invited addresses
invited lectures
lectures and colloquia
scholarly presentations
programs and workshops
professional activities
presentation and publications
abstracts
publications
scholarly publications
scholarly works
works in progress
bibliography
books
chapters
editorial boards
professional papers
technical papers
refereed journal articles
editorial appointments
articles/monographs

consulting experience
consultantships
continuing education experience
related experiences
academic service
advising
profesisonal service
professional community service
professional development
university involvement

service
outreach
faculty leadersihp
major committees
committee leadership
departmental leadership
professional association advisory
  boards
major university assignments
advisory committees
national boards
conferences attended
conference participation
conference presentation
conference leadership
workshop presentation

scholarships
fellowships
academic awards
honors
distinctions
college distinctions
activities and distinctions
honors and awards
professional recognition
prizes
college activities
awards
affiliations
memberships
professional memberships
memberships in scholarly societies
professional organizations
honorary societies
professional societies

reviews
book reviews
multimedia materials
selected presentation
research awards
research grants
funded projects
grants and contracts
grant activity
patents
exhibits/exhibitions
arrangements/scores
performances
recitals

portfolio
recommendations
references
professional certification
certification
licensure
endorsements
special training

foreign study
academic study abroad
academic travel abroad
international projects
languages
languages competencies

dossier
credentials
placement file

One of the most significant types of entries in the CV is those for publications, papers, and performances. Other entries relate to teaching, service, academic and/or work experience, and miscellaneous activities. When writing individual CV entries, each entry should have at least three main divisions. Entries should be written using a bibliographic style prescribed for your discipline, e.g., APA (American Psychological Association), MLA (Modern Language Association), Chicago (based on style manual published by University of Chicago), CBE (Council of Biology Editors), etc. Insert at least one space between entries. The main divisions of an entry for a publication, conference paper, or performance include: (1) Presenter's/ Author's/ Artist's Name; (2) Title of Presentation/Paper/Performance; (3) Facts of Publication/ Paper/Performance; (4) Page Numbers (if applicable). For all types of entries, write your name in reverse order with your Last Name first and your First Name last. Book titles and artistic works should be underlined or italicized; enclose the titles of other works in quotation marks. The facts of the publication, paper, or performance should include the place or location of the publication, paper, or performance; name of publishing agency or venue or organization; date of publication, paper, or performance; and page numbers (#—#) for publications. Books or journals are to include Volume Number (v. ##), Issue Number (#.#.), and/or Series Number (#.#.#), if applicable. In general, for internet facts, after the date, include URL followed by date of access, in parentheses.

You may find it necessary to write brief descriptions of entries for academic, work, or other related experiences, presentations, performances, and exhibitions in the CV. Avoid passive words or phrases such as "responsible for" or "duties included" and use verbs, nouns, and adjectives when describing activity in your CV (see examples below). Sentence fragments are preferred using a bulleted list format; closing with a period is optional.

Action Words

VERBS	acquired	advised	articulated
abstracted	acted	analyzed	assessed
accomplished	addressed	arranged	assisted

authored	founded	prepared	volunteered
budgeted	generated	presented	wrote
catalogued	guided	presided	
chaired	identified	produced	**NOUNS**
coauthored	illustrated	programmed	achievement
collaborated	implemented	projected	ability
collected	improved	promoted	ambition
communicated	increased	published	competence
complied	initiated	recognized	confidence
completed	instructed	recruited	creativity
composed	integrated	represented	dedication
conducted	interpreted	researched	determination
consulted	interviewed	reviewed	development
coordinated	introduced	revised	diversity
counseled	invented	scheduled	economy
created	investigated	screened	excellence
delivered	lectured	selected	experience
designed	maintained	served	harmony
developed	managed	solved	honor
directed	mastered	sponsored	imagination
drafted	monitored	streamlined	ingenuity
earned	motivated	strengthened	judgment
edited	negotiated	studied	merit
elected	nominated	supervised	prestige
encouraged	observed	taught	recognition
established	organized	tested	retention
evaluated	originated	trained	success
examined	participated	translated	training
expanded	performed	tutored	
facilitated	planned	verified	

After the CV is created and used for a particular annual review or for tenure and promotion, it must be proofread, revised, and updated for new activities. Your CV should be revised and updated regularly (each month, at most — each semester, at the very least) to note a course, publication, presentation, new or continuing committee assignment, or

188

any professional development, and, etc. Major revisions of your CV should occur when significant changes transpire in your professional career such as promotions which result in new faculty ranks, e.g., doctoral candidate to instructor or lecturer; doctoral candidate to assistant professor; assistant professor to associate professor; associate professor to professor. This means that some categories/headings may need to be collapsed or expanded. For example, in the first year of a probationary faculty member's career, you may not have enough publications to list them separately from their presentations. A general header like "Publications and Presentations" would work fine. However, as each list grows, you will need to revise your CV and create a separate list for each category (Forno and Reed, 1999, p. 25). In order to update and revise your CV, a good record keeping system is necessary. Electronic records saved on the hard drive of your computer, organized by teaching, scholarship, and service would be helpful. Also, retaining hard copies of materials in file folders in a filing cabinet will be a good, dependable resource as long as you remember to place the copy of the conference program or committee appointment letter in the file folder as soon as you receive them.

The CV in its "final" state for submission is as important as writing and formatting it. The CV should be printed on white, 8½ by 11 inch, 20 pound (weight) office paper. White is the best color and 20 pound the best weight because this paper is easier to photocopy and is easier to read. Your CV should be spotless: if coffee stains, smeared ink, or extraneous marks are on it, print a new copy of the CV. CVs must be typewritten or word-processed, not hand-written. Some good font specifications include Times New Roman, Arial, Courier New, Courier, and Times because they are easier to read. Font sizes can range from 12-point-to-14-point. Use diverse font styles—bold, italics, underline, all capital letters—for CV section headings and categories. There is no page limit on the CV. A doctoral candidate's CV most likely begins at 2 pages and then increases as their career progresses. On the other hand, a senior Full Professor may have a CV as long as 30 single-typed pages.

Insert your full name or last name only and page numbers at the top right hand corner of your CV. Laser-print-outs of your CV will produce a clear sharp image so this is highly recommended. (Photocopies of a laser-printed version are okay, too.) University tenure and promotion committees may vary slightly in their requirements for submitting tenure and promotion materials. Normally, a CV should be stapled in the top left-hand corner. However, university tenure and promotion committees will most likely request hard copies of the CV and other materials in a 3-ring binder in which case, the CV should not be stapled. When the research or creative activity package that includes your CV and sample publications is mailed to external reviewers, the CV should be stapled and mailed in a 9 by 12 inch envelope (a CV or job application materials should never be submitted in a regular business-sized envelope).

Applying for tenure and promotion is a stressful, yet rewarding process in a probationary faculty color's career. Hopefully, becoming knowledgeable about and understanding the purpose and basics of writing a CV will assist in improving and strengthening your existing CV, therefore removing some of the stress from the process.

CV Template

FIRST NAME LAST NAME
Street Address
City, State, Zip Code+4
+1-###-###-#### [Telephone number]
###@###.### [E-mail address]
Personal Web Site URL (optional)

EDUCATION
• Ph.D., Specialization, Institution, Date of Degree (or Anticipated/ Expected Date).
• M.A./M.S./M.F.A./M.B.A./M.M.; Major, Minor, Emphasis, Concentration, Institution, Date of Degree.
• B.A./B.S./B.F.A/B.M.; Major, Minor; Institution, Date of Degree.

OTHER ACCREDITATIONS
• Type of Accreditation/Licensure/Registration, Institution Awarding Accreditation, Location (City, State), Date.

Ph.D. DISSERTATION
- Title, Advisor or Director Name
- Abstract summary (4–5 sentences) discussing content and methodology

ACADEMIC EXPERIENCE
- Job Title/Rank, Employer, Location (City, State), 20##–Present
- Top Proficiencies or Skills Used

OTHER ACADEMIC EXPERIENCE
- Job Title/Rank, Employer, Location (City, State), 20##–Present
- Top Proficiencies or Skills Used

TEACHING & RESEARCH OR SCHOLARLY & SERVICE INTERESTS
- Main Areas of Inquiry/Interest

COURSES TAUGHT (WITHOUT STUDENT RATINGS)
- Course Title, Section Number, Institution, Enrollment, Semester Year.

COURSES TAUGHT (WITH STUDENT RATINGS)
- Course Title, Section Number, Institution, Semester Year, Enrollment, Rating (as compared to maximum points) x.x/x.0, Number of students who completed evaluations (n=xx).

UNDERGRADUATE/GRADUATE STUDENT THESES, DISSERTATIONS, EXAMINATIONS
- Student Name, Thesis Title/Dissertation Title/Examination, Department, Semester Year

CURRICULUM DEVELOPMENT (courses including distance education), workshops, educational materials)
- Course Title, Institution (if different from current institution), Semester Year

OTHER FORMS OF TEACHING
- Institution (include if you have worked at more than one university)
- Role, Semester Year.

GRANTS AND CONTRACTS
- Last Name/First Name of Principal Investigator and/or Co-Principal

Investigator(s). "Title of Project," Funding Agency, Agency Project Number, Date, Dollar Amount.

PUBLICATIONS

- Last Name, First Name. "Title of Work," Name of Publication/Publisher (*Newsletter, Newspaper, Magazine, Journal, Book*), Location of Publisher (State & City or Major City), Date of Publication, Volume Number (v. ##), Issue Number (#.#.), Series Number (#.#.#), Page Numbers (#—#). Note: Use a bibliographic style prescribed for your discipline, e.g., APA, MLA, Chicago, CBE, etc. For internet publication/paper facts: After date, include URL followed by date of access, in parentheses.

PRESENTATIONS

- Last Name, First Name. "Title of Presentation," Organization, Location of Presentation (City, State), Date (20##–20##).
  - Optional synopsis of content and/or purpose of presentation, audience, results, etc.

PERFORMANCES, EXHIBITIONS, DESIGNS, PATENTS

- Last Name, First Name. "Title," Role, Sponsor/Producer, Location (City, State), Date.
- Last Name, First Name. "Title of Patent." Patent Number, Date. Principal Creator/Designer and/or Co-Creator Designer(s).
- Last Name, First Name. "Title of Product or Engineering Design." Company Accepting Design, Location (City, State), Date. Principal Engineer and/or Co-Principal Engineer(s).
  - Provide optional description of product, audience, function, etc.

SERVICE TO THE UNIVERSITY

- Institution (include if you have worked at more than one university)
- Role, Committee, Date/Semester Year.

SERVICE TO THE DEPARTMENT/DIVISION/SCHOOL

- Institution (include if you have worked at more than one university)
- Role, Committee, Date/Semester Year.

SERVICE TO THE PROFESSION

- Institution (include if you have worked at more than one university)
- Role, Committee, Date/Semester Year.

SERVICE TO THE COMMUNITY
- Institution (include if you have worked at more than one university)
- Role, Committee, Date/Semester Year.

PROFESSIONAL AND SCHOLARLY ORGANIZATIONS MEMBER-SHIPS/AFFILIATIONS
- Society, Organization, or Association Name, Position Held, 19##–20##

HONORS, AWARDS AND ACHIEVEMENTS AND OTHER SPECIAL COMMENDATIONS
- *Title of Award, Sponsoring Institution/Organization, Date.*

PROFESSIONAL DEVELOPMENT OR CONTINUING EDUCATION EXPERIENCES (courses, workshops, improvement leaves, post-doctoral training)

PROFESSIONAL DEVELOPMENT OR CONTINUING EDUCATION PRESENTATIONS

RESEARCH OR PROFESSIONAL CONSULTANTSHIPS

STUDY ABROAD AND/OR LANGUAGE COMPETENCIES (include scholarly, academic travel only)

REFERENCES/RECOMMENDATIONS (list 3–4 references willing to write recommendation letters; include complete contact information)
- *Name, Title; Institutional Affiliation; Address; City, State, Zip Code; Area Code, Office Phone Number*

CREDENTIALS (provide address where recipient can access your career/placement file)
- *Name, Title; Institutional Affiliation; Address; City, State, Zip Code; Area Code, Office Phone Number*

REFERENCES

Anthony, R., and G. Roe. (1998). *The curriculum vitae handbook: Presenting and promoting your academic career.* 2d ed. San Francisco: Rudi.
Anthony, R., and G. Roe. (1994). *The curriculum vitae handbook: Using your CV to present and promote your academic career.* Iowa City, IA: Rudi.

Chronicle of Higher Education. Career network. http://chronicle.com/jobs.

Formo, D. M., and C. Reed. (1999). *Job search in academe: Strategic rhetoric for faculty job candidates.* Sterling, VA: Stylus.

Heiberger, M. M., and J. M. Vick. (2001). *The academic job search handbook.* 3d ed. Philadelphia: University of Pennsylvania Press.

Hume, K. (2005). *Surviving your academic job hunt: Advice for humanities Ph.D.s.* New York: Palgrave.

Jackson, A. L. (1999). *How to prepare your curriculum vitae.* New York: McGraw-Hill.

Kronenfeld, J. J., and M. L. Whicker. (1997). *Getting an academic job: Strategies for success.* Thousand Oaks, CA: Sage.

McCabe, L. L. and E. R. B. McCabe. (2000). *How to succeed in academics.* San Diego, CA: Academic Press.

Showalter, E., H. Figler, L. G. Kletzer, J. H. Schuster, and S. R. Katz. (1996). *The MLA guide to the job search: A handbook for departments and Ph.D.s and Ph.D. candidates in English and foreign languages.* New York: Modern Language Association of America.

Sowers-Hoag, K., and D. F. Harrison. (1998). *Finding an academic job.* Thousand Oaks, CA: Sage.

Thompson, M. A. (2000). *The global resume and CV guide.* New York: Wiley.

Life After Tenure Denial

ANDREA SMITH

When professors get a tenure-track job, their focus tends to be on earning tenure. As a junior faculty person at the University of Michigan, the consistent message I heard not only from senior colleagues at my institution, but others in the academy across the country, was I should drop everything else that was going on in my life and spend the next six years focused on getting sufficient numbers of publications to secure tenure. Tenure is framed as the most important professional achievement — if it does not come to fruition, our lives will be completely devastated. We cannot imagine life after tenure denial. To illustrate, when I attended my first academic conference as a master's student, a speaker on a mentoring panel told the story of one of her colleagues who committed suicide over her negative tenure decision. I do not know who this person was and hence do not know the specifics leading to her tragic decision. But what seemed to me to compound the tragedy of this story was the fact that it was told as if this was a normal response to tenure denial. The storyteller explained why we need to make sure people of color achieve tenure. She did not question why the response to tenure denial would lead to suicide. There was no discussion or questioning of why tenure should loom so large in our lives in the first place. At that moment I vowed to myself I was not going to fully invest in the tenure process to the point that I would be willing to kill myself over it. And as I continued along my academic career, I began to see the need to do more than develop individualized responses to the pressures of academia. It is not enough to survive the oppressive mechanisms of the academic

195

industrial complex, it is important to develop collective strategies to dismantle these devices.

As it so happens, I failed to earn tenure at my first job at the University of Michigan. I had two books, two edited anthologies, two edited special journal issues, fourteen peer reviewed articles, and twenty-five book chapters. I purportedly had excellent external reviews as well as the most academic publications and one of the best teaching records of my cohorts going up for tenure in both of my departments that year. I had essentially done everything I was supposed to do to get tenure, but I still lost my tenure case. While I cannot say being denied tenure was pleasant at the time, in retrospect, its impact on my life has been relatively minor. I think the reason is that, during my tenure battle, I remembered the promise I had made to myself to not over-invest in the tenure process. I also recalled a decision I had made earlier in my career when I was involved in racial justice struggle as a master's of divinity student at Union Theological Seminary at the same time this institution was considering my application for doctoral studies. I wondered if I should withdraw my involvement so as not to jeopardize my application. I decided then that I had to ask myself the question, what is more important to me, ending global oppression or securing academic success? While, ideally it would be nice to achieve both, I had to make my priority the former. Thus, when I was denied tenure, I remembered that this was part of a life-decision I had made, to struggle for things I believe in, knowing that sometimes I would pay the cost. On the positive side, it is crises like these that further demonstrate the importance of being tied to larger movements so that one does not suffer these kinds of injustices alone. The widespread support I did receive enabled me to find employment at another university, where I did receive tenure soon thereafter.

In cases like mine, it is easy to focus on the specifics of what happened at my particular institution. What was the political environment like? What explained the lack of support from senior colleagues? What was it about my work that some colleagues found threatening? In other words, the question that comes up first is what was wrong with that particular institution/department? However, while there were certainly problematic dynamics at the University of Michigan, I do not think it is particularly worse than any other academic institution. That is because

I do not think my case was an exceptional case, but is a reflection of the business-as-usual politics of the academic industrial complex. Our jobs would be much easier if our problems were confined to individual racist and/or sexist departments and universities. We could just target them specifically. Unfortunately, however, our problem is not racism *within* universities; our problem is that the university is itself structured by the logics of white supremacy, colonialism and capitalism.

Rather than view the university as a benign institution, it is more correctly understood as an ideological state apparatus designed to reify the settler colonialist, white supremacist and capitalist status quo. It is fundamentally a capitalist institution because it is premised on the assumption that education is a commodity that should be bought and sold on the academic market place. Consequently, not all peoples are entitled to quality education; only those who can afford it. However, the academy also functions as an ideological state apparatus; the academy must disavow its complicity in capitalism by claiming itself as a system based solely on meritocracy. That is, the students who advance do so, not because they have more resources, but because they are smarter. Similarly, those employed in the academic industrial complex advance because they are smarter than their colleagues. Even progressives within the academy tend to perpetuate this myth of meritocracy by their refusal to see academia as a game whose rules anyone can learn to play strategically. This is why even radical thinkers are so devastated after tenure denial because they believe this denial demonstrates that they are less smart or less deserving of recognition than their colleagues.

This culture of meritocracy then compels professors in the academy to work tirelessly (or at least give the appearance of working tirelessly), because if they do not appear to be working 24 hours a day, they fear they will be condemned as being a lazy or an undeserving scholar. I, for instance, have been told on innumerable occasions that if I have time to do as much activist work as I do, I must not really be doing scholarship. But if we do support social justice, then we should be demystifying the academy rather than perpetuating its capitalist logics. The reality is, one does not have to work tirelessly to be successful in academia. Rather than always feeling compelled to promote the appearance of busyness in our lives, we should demystify the academy and share strategies of how to manage it effectively.

If we start to realize that academia is not a meritocracy, then we are less likely to be fooled by the lie that we need to dispense with our lives in order to do quality scholarship. Why has being a good scholar and academic come to mean that one should be working incessantly at the expense of doing social justice work, having fun, or maintaining interests outside academia? It is not sufficient to ask ourselves, how can we lead more balanced lives? Or, how can we balance a life of social justice activism with a job in academia? Rather, we must deconstruct the logic of the academic industrial complex to see how it has needlessly trapped us into thinking that we must choose between academia and having a life.

It is rare that even radical scholars challenge the terms of the debate within the academic system, even as they complain about it. Progressives who turn a critical eye to all the other institutions in society often seem to unwittingly assume the academy is either a neutral or benevolent institution that simply needs changes in personnel or different policies and procedures. Because the actual structure of the academy goes unquestioned—from tenure processes, to grading systems, to academic hierarchies, even progressives get trapped in the academy's myth of meritocracy that either makes them insane or turns them into fascists. All the collective action we support outside the academy seems to disappear inside it—as we slave away in our offices in order to make sure everyone knows how busy and hardworking we are. Instead, we could be working together to support each other, build community, demystify the academic industrial complex, swap survival strategies and promote life for all of us. If we did that, then tenure could no longer function as the weapon it currently does to discipline us into the capitalist and colonialist logics of the academic industrial complex. For instance, if we no longer believed that the academy was a meritocracy premised on the foundation of individual "genius," we might more readily engage in collective work, such as collective teaching, research and advising. All knowledge production is collective anyway, so rather than position colleagues as competitors, we could see ourselves as collaborators. This would then free up our time to have fulfilling lives.

In addition, the myth of meritocracy often contributes to not only intellectual, but political isolation. That is, because we are supposed to prove our individual worth, we see other people as competitors rather than allies. When things like tenure denial happen to us, we feel individually shamed rather than recognize these actions as emanating from the logics of a capitalist system. Consequently, we also deal with repercussions of these things alone rather than with other people. I was struck by how many times during not only my case, but the cases of others who were denied tenure, that we were told not to tell anyone. We should keep our tenure denial a secret because otherwise the world would know of our academic unworthiness. And I am also stunned with how many people do keep these traumatic experiences secret. The end result is to deny us both emotional and political support.

In times like these, it is important to remember that political action must be collective to be effective. The system can handle thousands of oppositional academics as long as they do not work together. It is only when we act collectively that our political power becomes a threat to the system. Or, as New Orleans activist Barbara Major (2003) argues: "When you go to power without a base, your demand becomes a request." That is why it is essential for women of color in the academy in particular to engage in collective organizing, not only among our colleagues, but the broader community outside of our institutions. We will be protected when the institution knows it is going to face serious repercussions and condemnation from as many people as possible should it choose to undermine us.

The other consequence of the logics of meritocracy is not only do we doubt our academic self-worth when we are not included in the system, but we become gatekeepers when we are included. Academia works not just to exclude women of color, but also to selectively include them. Unfortunately, as Rey Chow notes, the assumption that the system is unfair when it excludes me tends to give rise to the assumption that if the system does include me, then it must be fair (Chow, 2002, p. 180). In fact, the system is not fair when it includes or excludes. The system also selectively provides the veneer that it is fair. Those who then get included feel so honored by this inclusion that they become the gatekeepers for the institution because they feel invested in its fairness. In my experience, I have certainly faced exclusion, such as my tenure denial. But I have also been included and given opportunities that other people deserved more than I did. The system was no more fair when I was included than when I was excluded. In most of the cases I have seen, tenure denial of women of color is usually enabled by other women of color functioning as gatekeepers.

Finally, because those of us in the academy have deeply internalized its myth of meritocracy, we have also internalized the notion that academics somehow are more special or important than other workers. Again, we look at tenure processes as being about the worth of not only one's intellectual work, but one's worth as a human being. Instead, we should more properly look at tenure as a labor issue. To do so, we would then see ourselves as workers who, like all other workers, need to organize to secure more equitable working conditions. Instead of fighting just to advance particular tenure cases, we could organize to change the conditions of tenure itself as an issue of workers' rights. Reframing tenure issues as labor issues then might enable us to work collaboratively with other struggles, including those workers in the academy who are the most economically vulnerable. Doing so would further our ability to build political power that would ensure greater job security for all of us in the future.

Thus, when we reframe the issues of tenure, we realize that the patterns of racism and sexism that manifest themselves in tenure processes are not sharply distinct from the racial and gender logics of the capitalist system in general. Consequently, our strategies to address the trials of tenure must go beyond cultivating individual survival skills. The capitalist logics of the academic industrial complex compel us to engage the academy as individuals who need to prove their "merit." As Native studies scholar Glen Coulthard notes, our responses to conditions of oppression is often not to dismantle structures of oppression, but to seek recognition from those structures (Coulthard, 2007). Thus, we spend our energy trying to get the worth of our work recognized, or the work of genders studies, queer studies, ethnic studies, indigenous studies, etc., recognized as valuable by the academy. But we should be clear that our only real value to the academic industrial complex is to add what Elizabeth Povinelli (2002) describes as "social difference without social consequence"

(p. 16). Our value is to provide a multicultural alibi to the white suprem-acy and capitalist logics of the academy. In the end, we will never really be legitimate in the academic industrial complex except insofar as to serve as gatekeepers to stop other women of color being in the academy.

Thus, rather than seeking the ever-elusive recognition, our work conditions are much more likely to improve once we transform the cur-rent white supremacist, colonial, heteropatriarchal, and capitalist system itself. To do so, we must put tenure within the larger context of social justice struggle and engage in collective action in order to gain political power so that we can actually change the system. One such group, the recently formed Critical Ethnic Studies Association, has organized for this very reason. Rather than seeking multicultural representation within the academy, CESA aims to connect ethnic studies with broad move-ments for social change in order to transform the academy as we know it. As its mission statement articulates:

> The Critical Ethnic Studies Association (CESA) aims to develop an approach to scholarship, institution building, and activism animated by the spirit of the decolonial, antiracist, and other global liberationist move-ments that enabled the creation of Ethnic Studies, and which continues to inform its political and intellectual projects. We seek to move away from current critical deadlocks, to counteract institutional marginalization, to revisit the political ideas that precipitated ethnic studies' founding moment within the U.S. academy, and to create new conversations.

> **Our vision:**

> Ethnic studies scholarship has laid the foundation for analyzing how racism, settler colonialism, immigration, imperialism, and slavery interact in the creation and maintenance of systems of domination, dispossession, criminalization, expropriation, exploitation, and violence that are predi-cated upon hierarchies of racialized, gendered, sexualized, economized, and nationalized social existence in the United States and beyond. Our vision of Critical Ethnic Studies highlights how systematized oppression is coterminous with the multitude of practices that resist these systems.

> Some ethnic studies paradigms have become entrapped within, and some-times indistinguishable from, the mandates of liberal multiculturalism, which rely on a politics of identitarian representation beholden to U.S. nation-building and capitalist imperatives. On the one hand, as ethnic studies has become more legitimized within the academy, it has frequently done so by distancing itself from those very international social movements that were the triggers for its genesis. On the other hand, ethnic studies

201

departments have always existed at the periphery of the academic industrial complex in the university undercommons, but they have been further marginalized through funding cuts in the wake of the 2008 global economic crisis. Interrogating the limitations of ethnic studies today and counteracting these appropriations, the Critical Ethnic Studies Association (CESA) has as its central goal the development of an approach to scholarship, institution building, and activism that is animated by the spirit of the decolonial, antiracist, and other global liberationist movements that enabled the creation of Ethnic Studies (Asian American Studies, Black Studies, Native American Studies, Arab-American Studies, Latino/a Studies, and Postcolonial Studies) and continues to inform its political and intellectual projects. We do this to move away from current critical deadlocks, to counteract institutional marginalization, to revisit the political ideas that precipitated ethnic studies' founding moment within the U.S. academy, and to create new conversations. However, far from advocating the peremptory dismissal of identity or the wholesale embrace of identitarian nationalism, CESA seeks to construct an open dialogue around white supremacy, settler colonialism, capitalism, and heteropatriarchy, as well as militarism, occupation, indigeneity, neocolonialism, anti-immigration, anti–Islam, etc. in order to expand the conceptual parameters and transformative capacities of ethnic studies. An un-disciplinary formation, critical ethnic studies has decolonization not as its goal but sees decolonizing as a set of ongoing theories, practices, imaginaries, and methods in the service of abolishing global oppression. Thus, rather than focusing exclusively on critique, critical ethnic studies stands for decolonizing as a generative praxis of worldmaking.

While CESA does not romanticize social movements or prescribe a specific relationship between scholars and activists, we seek to call into question the emphasis on professionalization within ethnic studies and the concomitant refusal to interrogate the politics of the academic industrial complex or to engage with broader movements for social transformation. Critical ethnic studies, while building bridges beyond the academy, locates itself within the neoliberal university as a site of contestation and as part of the struggle over the political, economic, cultural, etc. structures of the world that we inhabit. We do this to counteract the tendency of seeing the academic industrial complex as radically removed from the world and to situate the university as one location among many for political struggles. Irrefutable as the evidence is of the university's enmeshment in governmental and corporate structures, ethnic studies has at times been structurally complicit in neutralizing the university rather than interrogating how the university transforms ideas into ideology, thought into action, and knowledge into power.

CESA is an inclusive organization that invites the participation of ethnic studies scholars and students from different generations, academic disciplines, and geographical locations. CESA is committed to these practices in its administrative configuration, which, instead of having a hierarchical structure, avoids the trappings of traditional organizations and consists of a shifting collective with changing coordinators that encourages the participation and initiative of local affiliates, initiatives, etc. CESA is a loosely networked organization that provides a forum for thinking about global variants of racialization, racial and colonial domination, capital, heteropatriarchy, and settler colonialism through biannual conferences, a journal, and various local initiatives.

The Critical Ethnic Studies Association understands the intellectual, activist, and institutional practices within its purview as tools in the imagination and construction of a better, more just world ["CESA Vision"].

For those who are committed to social justice, it is important to remember that even if we do not get tenure, no institution can stop us from continuing to engage in broader liberation struggles and engaging in the intellectual work necessary to support these struggles. The university does not own intellectual work. And for those of who do ethnic studies, indigenous studies, gender studies, etc., this work is most certainly not owned by the academic industrial complex. These intellectual projects arose from movements against white supremacy, heteropatriarchy, settler colonialism, etc. While the university has often co-opted these projects, we do not need to let this co-optation continue. In our efforts to gain "respectability" for these projects, we often cut ourselves off from the very movements that allowed these projects to be in the university in the first place, and hence we cut ourselves off from our source of power. Thus, ethnic studies, for instance, happens when and wherever we decide to engage in the intellectual and political work of dismantling white supremacy. We are not dependent on holding academic jobs to do this work. When we then invest in what makes us passionate in life, we can then work within the academic industrial complex to further our passions. At the same time, our passions are not reducible to the academy. If we don't get tenure, we can still pursue our passions rather than make tenure survival the only thing we feel passionate about.

References

Chow, R. (2002). *The Protestant ethnic and the spirit of capitalism*. New York: Columbia University Press.

Coulthard, G. (2007). Subjects of empire: Indigenous peoples and the "politics of recognition" in Canada. *Contemporary Political Theory, 6*(4), 437–460.

Critical Ethnic Studies Association. *Critical ethnic studies vision*. Retrieved on March 5, 2012, from criticalethnicstudies.org.

Major, B. (2003, June). When you go to power without a base, your demand becomes a request. Keynote Speech presented at the National Women's Studies Association National Conference, New Orleans, Louisiana.

Provinelli, E. (2002). *The cunning of recognition: Indigenous alterities and the making of Australian multiculturalism*. Durham, NC: Duke University Press.

About the Contributors

Michelle Madsen **Camacho** is chair of the Sociology Department and affiliated faculty with the Ethnic Studies Department and Women's and Gender Studies Program at the University of San Diego. Her research examines racial and gender inequities in STEM education. Her research has been published by numerous journals including *Latino Studies, Journal of Engineering Education, Journal of Women and Minorities in Science and Engineering; Journal of Hispanics in Higher Education*. In 2011 she was named the McNair Mentor of the Year and also received the award for Innovative and Experiential Teaching Excellence.

Robin R. Means **Coleman** is an associate professor in the Department of Communication Studies at the University of Michigan. She also holds a joint appointment with the Department for Afro-American and African Studies. Coleman is the author of *African-American Viewers and the Black Situation Comedy: Situating Racial Humor* and *Horror Noire: Blacks in American Horror Films from the 1890s to Present*. She is the editor of *Say It Loud! African American Audiences, Media, and Identity* and coeditor of *Fight the Power! The Spike Lee Reader*, and has published numerous book chapters and journal articles.

Alyssa **Garcia** is an assistant professor of women's studies at Pennsylvania State University. Her teaching and research interests include Latin American and Caribbean studies, Latina/o studies, critical race theory, and feminist ethnography. Publications include "Continuous Moral Economies: The State Regulation of Bodies and Sex-Work in Cuba," *Sexualities* (2010); "Situating Race, Navigating Belonging: Mapping Afro-Cuban Identities in the U.S.," *Latina/o Research Review* (2009); and "Counter-Stories of Race and Gender: Situating the Experiences of Latinas in the Academe," *Latino Studies Journal* (2005).

Toni **Griego Jones** is an associate professor in the Department of Teaching, Learning and Sociocultural Studies at the University of Arizona. Her research focuses on teacher preparation for Latino students and Latino parent involvement in education of their children. She has authored many journal articles and chapters on these topics and coauthored the book *Teaching Hispanic Children.*

Samuel D. **Henry** is an associate professor of education in the Graduate School of Education at Portland State University. He also serves on the State of Oregon School Board and the Oregon Education Investment Board. He has served in a number of civic capacities and in multiple university leadership positions over a four decade career in education, with scholarly work on desegregation, cultural pluralism, and culture contact, educational reform, international education, and policy and politics in education.

Tasneem **Khaleel** is dean of the College of Arts and Sciences and professor of biology at Montana State University Billings. She also served as director of Graduate Studies and Research (1993–96) and chair of the Department of Biological and Physical Sciences (1996–2004). She was the first woman to receive a Ph.D. from Bangalore University, South India (in 1970). Her research has focused on cytotaxonomy/plant reproductive biology. Recent publications include "Estradiol distribution during the development and expression of reproductive structures in *Populus tremuloides* (Micx.)" in *Sexual Plant Reproduction* (2003).

Judith **Liu** is a professor of sociology at the University of San Diego; affiliated faculty in the Department of Ethnic Studies; and Faculty Liaison in the Center for Community Service Learning. Her latest book is *Foreign Exchange: Counterculture Behind the Walls of St. Hilda's School for Girls, 1929–1937*, and she is the coauthor of *Contested Terrain: Diversity, Writing, and Knowledge*, and *The Ethnographic Eye: Interpretive Studies of Education in China*. She is the author/coauthor of numerous articles and book chapters on women and HIV; education in China; and community service-learning.

Dwayne **Mack** is an associate professor of history and affiliated faculty with African and African American studies at Berea College in Berea, Kentucky, where he holds the Carter G. Woodson Chair in African American History. He is the author of several articles and book chapters on the African American experience in the West and South. His work in progress includes "We Have a Story to Tell: The African American Community in Spokane, Washington, 1945–1990."

Juliet **McMullin** is an associate professor of anthropology at the University of California Riverside. She is the author of *The Healthy Ancestor: Embodied Inequality and the Revitalization of Native Hawaiian Health* and contributor and editor of the School for Advanced Research volume *Confronting Cancer: Metaphors, Advocacy, and Anthropology*. She has published numerous articles on health inequalities and community-based participatory research.

Angela M. **Nelson** is an associate professor in the Department of Popular Culture at Bowling Green State University. She has presented or copresented numerous faculty development workshops and seminars about the curriculum vita. She has edited *"This Is How We Flow": Rhythm in Black Cultures* and coedited *Popular Culture Theory and Methodology: A Basic Introduction*.

Tom **Otieno** is an associate dean in the College of Arts and Sciences and professor of chemistry at Eastern Kentucky University. His research involves the synthesis of various classes of transition metal complexes, determination of their properties, and the correlation of these properties with their structures. In addition to coauthoring numerous scientific publications, he has also published articles in the areas of academic leadership, faculty development, and university/ K–12 partnerships.

Mark A. **Pottinger** is an associate professor of music history and chair of the Department of Fine Arts at Manhattan College in New York City. He is the author of several publications on the music and cultural life of 19th-century France, including *The Staging of History in France*. He is writing "Romantic Science: Nineteenth-Century Opera in the Age of Becoming," examining the pan–European Romantic aesthetic and its relationship to opera, history and the burgeoning profession of science in the first half of the 19th century.

Andrea **Smith** is an associate professor at the University of California, Riverside, in the Department of Media and Cultural Studies. Her publications include *Native Americans and the Christian Right: The Gendered Politics of Unlikely Alliances* and *Conquest: Sexual Violence and American Indian Genocide*. She is also the editor of *The Revolution Will Not Be Funded: Beyond the Nonprofit Industrial Complex* and co-editor of *The Color of Violence, The Incite! Anthology*. She is a co-founder of Incite! Women of Color Against Violence. She recently completed a report for the United Nations on indigenous peoples and boarding schools.

Jacqueline B. **Temple** is an associate professor of teacher education in the Graduate School of Education at Portland State University. She is a Fulbright alumna and director of the International Teacher Education Licensure Program and has authored numerous articles and book chapters on the intersections of inclusion, social justice and teacher education.

Yer J. **Thao** is an associate professor of education in the Department of Curriculum and Instruction at Portland State University in Portland, Oregon. He teaches multicultural and bilingual education and current issues in education and society. With research interests including ethnic identity, teacher training, linguistic diversity and oral tradition, he is the author of *The Mong Oral Tradition: Cultural Memory in the Absence of Written Language*.

Elwood D. **Watson** is a professor of history, African American studies and gender studies at East Tennessee State University. He is the author of several scholarly articles, editor of four anthologies, coeditor of three anthologies and is the author of *Outsiders Within: Black Women in The Legal Academy After Brown v. Board*. He is also a blogger for *Diverse Education, X/Y Online and The Black Past.org*.

Index

① What are we asking pre-retention
   faculty to do? Committee
   etc.

② Are there differences based on
   identities?

③ What is fair in the form of retention
   eg expectations?

Quote by Maxine Greene

p. 140
   → critical Theory
        AND
   Action for social change.

ps. 140
What is presumed?

School experience:

Confluence of: 1. culture(s)
2. Curricula
3. organizational behavior
4. Student's selfhood

overcome personally AND institutionally

① Access to informal networks (32)
② Workload — Invisible task (35-36)
AND
— The "Diversity Ask"

① Co-cultural oppression (44)
② nanny / Mammy Syndrome (47-48)
③ Evaluation (50) — actual practice —
great example!

① Which courses are supported? e.g. → 3 in Latino boo
would we do the same for Latin American? Black Experience?
(73) Which courses are subject to who w/ fact — which
Stand no matter however?

Cultural taxation — expectation of service for
diversity Sake — (75)

Mentoring — (78-79) ⇒ National Center for Faculty
Development and Diversity

Lorde quote (85)

PS 122 COMMITTEE Review Materials
How do we recognize the Complexity
and load of FOC in Retention
process?
How do we celebrate accomplishments?